SPINOZA

BENEDICTUS DE SPINOZA.

Dit is de schaduw van SPINOZA's zienlijk beelt,
Daar 't gladde koper geen sieraat meer aan kon geven;
Maar zijn GEZEGENT brein, zoo rijk hem meêgedeelt,
Doet in zijn SCHRIFTEN hem aanschouwen naar het leven.
Wie oit BEGEERTE TOT DE WYSHEIT heeft gehad,
Hier was die zuiver en op 't snedigste gevat.

Spinoza

Freedom's Messiah

———◆❙◆❙◆———

IAN BURUMA

Yale
UNIVERSITY
PRESS

New Haven and London

Yale University Press books may be purchased in quantity for
educational, business, or promotional use. For information, please email
sales.press@yale.edu (U.S. office) or sales@yaleup.co.uk (U.K. office).

Set in Janson Oldstyle type by Integrated Publishing Solutions.
Printed in the United States of America.

Library of Congress Control Number: 2023941204
ISBN 978-0-300-24892-0 (hardcover : alk. paper)

A catalogue record for this book is available from the British Library.

This paper meets the requirements of ANSI/NISO Z39.48-1992
(Permanence of Paper).

10 9 8 7 6 5 4 3 2

Frontispiece: Engraving of Spinoza commissioned
by his friends around 1680. Artist unknown.

ALSO BY IAN BURUMA

Behind the Mask: On Sexual Demons, Sacred Mothers, Transvestites, Gangsters, Drifters and Other Japanese Cultural Heroes (1984)

God's Dust: A Modern Asian Journey (1988)

The Wages of Guilt: Memories of War in Japan and Germany (1995)

The Missionary and the Libertine: Love and War in East and West (1996)

Anglomania: A European Love Affair (1999)

Bad Elements: Among the Rebels, Dissidents, and Democrats of Greater China (2001)

Inventing Japan: 1853–1964 (2003)

Occidentalism: The West in the Eyes of Its Enemies (2004)

Conversations with John Schlesinger (2006)

Murder in Amsterdam: The Death of Theo Van Gogh and the Limits of Tolerance (2006)

Taming the Gods: Religion and Democracy on Three Continents (2010)

Grenzen aan de vrijheid: Van De Sade tot Wilders (2010)

Year Zero: A History of 1945 (2013)

Theater of Cruelty (2014)

Their Promised Land: My Grandparents in Love and War (2016)

A Tokyo Romance (2018)

The Churchill Complex: The Curse of Being Special, from Winston and FDR to Trump and Brexit (2020)

The Collaborators: Three Stories of Deception and Survival in World War II (2023)

Novels:
Playing the Game (1990)
The China Lover (2008)

Photography Books:
The Japanese Tattoo (1980)
Spektakel in Tokio (2023)

For Leon Botstein

CONTENTS

SPINOZA

1

Everyone's Spinoza

> I never yet knew (said an Englishman extensively
> acquainted with the Literature and Literary Men of the
> North of Europe) a single person, whom Spinoza had ever
> converted to his way of thinking; but I know half a dozen at
> least who have converted Spinoza to theirs!
> —*Samuel Taylor Coleridge*

THE BONES OF Benedict or Baruch or Bento Spinoza are buried in the grounds of a handsome Dutch baroque Protestant church in The Hague. One way to the church in Spinoza's time was by boat through canals that no longer exist. But his body was carried to the New Church in 1677 in a funeral cortege of considerable pomp: six coaches followed his coffin, and distinguished figures from The Hague and Amsterdam are said to have arrived for the occasion. Two of the mourners might have been his sister (or possibly half-sister) Rebecca and his nephew Daniel. If so, they were the only Jews. Their presence would have been unusual. Since Spinoza had been cast out and cursed by his Portuguese synagogue in 1656, no Jew could "communicate with him orally or in writing, nor provide him any favor, nor be with him under the same roof, nor be within four cubits of him, nor read any paper composed or written by him."[1]

As though to make amends for the ban, or *herem*, a tombstone was erected in the churchyard in 1956 by admirers with the Hebrew word *amcha*, or "your people," engraved under the face of Spinoza carved out in white basalt. At the foot of the memorial lies a stone slab with words in Latin confirming that Spinoza's bones lie under this patch of earth. They had been buried inside before, but, possibly because the money to keep them there ran out, they were later moved outside with the remains of other people.

Whether or not Spinoza would have been happy to be received rather belatedly by "his people" we cannot know. Although he never converted to Christianity, or any other faith, he probably wouldn't have minded being buried among Protestants, with whom he had friendly relations, so long as they weren't orthodox Calvinists who denounced his books as the devil's work. And yet, as one might expect, Spinoza would remain a Jew in the eyes of most gentiles, including ones who were sympathetic to him. Christiaan Huygens, the great astronomer, inventor of the pendulum clock, and grandee from a family of grandees, called his learned friend "the Jew of Voorburg"— Voorburg being the place where Spinoza lived for a time.[2] Huygens spoke less as a racist than with the typical condescension of his class.

A request was made in 2012 to lift the ban on Spinoza. After all, it was argued, the *herem* seemed out of date in a society where free speech is considered a basic human right, and Spinoza was one of the greatest philosophers of all time. Various scholarly opinions were considered by the chief rabbi of the Portuguese synagogue in Amsterdam. But Dr. Pinchas Toledano concluded that there was no way he could possibly rescind the ban, since Spinoza had never repented, was buried on Christian ground, and besides, he said, the right to free speech did not extend to spreading heresies and denying the existence of God the creator.

The house where Spinoza died of consumption is about a five-minute walk from the New Church in a street still named Paviljoensgracht, after the canal that once ran along it. It is a handsome three-story house, not grand, but in the fine, sober seventeenth-century Dutch taste. A gray stone plaque in the russet brick façade tells us that Spinoza lived there from 1671 until 1677. The shutters on the graceful windows, as well as the woodwork inside, would then have been painted a dark mossy green. They have been restored to something similar today. During World War Two, when the Nazi occupiers had requisitioned the house, Spinoza's name was deleted from the plaque and replaced by the date on which the house was built, 1646. Spinoza lived on the top floor, and slept in his parents' bed, which was his only heirloom. His landlord, a painter and decorator named Hendrick van der Spyck, lived on the ground floor with his wife, Ida, and their children.

It would have been a raffish neighborhood in Spinoza's time, but with flashes of high style, not unlike the part of Amsterdam in which he grew up. Poor Ashkenazi Jews, who served the richer Sephardic merchants as servants in wealthier parts of town, lived there. But there were also some well-known artists. Paulus Potter, famous for his paintings of pastoral scenes featuring large bulls and fat, grazing cows, lived around the corner in the 1640s in a beautiful house that testified to his worldly success. It is still there today. I used to play in Potter's old house as a child, when it was owned by a well-known printer, whose son was a schoolmate of mine. I was entirely oblivious then of its rich history.

The man who built Spinoza's last house was another celebrated painter, mostly of landscapes, called Jan van Goyen. A very prolific artist, he lost a great deal of money when the mania for speculating on the price of tulips crashed in a disastrous slump in 1637, five years after Spinoza's birth. This only made Van Goyen more prolific. He sold the house to his son-in-law Havick Steen, son of Jan Steen, one of the most famous painters of the Dutch Golden Age, known for his pictures of drunken scenes in taverns or chaotic households.

Today, the Paviljoensgracht is still a little raffish, even though gentrification lends it a veneer of chic. The front window of Spinoza's old lodgings looks out onto a narrow street lined with the red lights of rooms rented by prostitutes, many of them from Africa, South America, or the poorer Balkan countries. Solitary men saunter up and down, taking their time. Between the street of red lights and the nearby railway station is an area populated mostly by North African and Turkish immigrants. There are halal butchers, kebab joints, and shops selling waterpipes. On the other side, behind the house, lies the modest Chinatown. Although he would no doubt be astonished by much of what he would see, Spinoza might still recognize some of his old neighborhood. The mix of bohemians and immigrants would have a familiar air.

It was only in the nineteenth century that people paid any attention to the house on the Paviljoensgracht. The first plaque identifying the house as the place where Spinoza once lived was installed in 1880. The canal was drained in 1900. In 1926 there was still a café with a billiards room on the ground floor. The house was bought by the Spinoza Society—the Domus Spinozana Society, to be exact—in 1927, with the intention of turning it into a center of Spinoza scholarship, with a museum and a library. This was still its function when I visited the house in the fall of 2021—at least on the ground floor, where Spinoza's landlord did his work. There was a small exhibition of prints showing Spinoza and Gottfried Wilhelm Leibniz having a conversation (no doubt in Latin; Spinoza had no German, and Leibniz would not have spoken Portuguese or Dutch). Leibniz visited The Hague in 1676 on his way from London to Hanover, where the duke of Brunswick had offered him a position. There was also a display of seventeenth-century editions of Spinoza's *Theological-Political Treatise* (Tractatus theologico-politicus) (1670) and his *Ethics* (Ethica, ordine geometrico demonstrata) (1677). Translations of Spinoza's works in many languages graced one bookcase, and scholarly books on his philosophy another. A courteous librarian told me that the Spinoza Society would love to take possession of the whole house, but that, alas, Spinoza's old rooms were still occupied by someone who was reluctant to sell.

The same librarian also told me about an old rivalry with a different Spinoza society that had been established in another house where Spinoza once lived, from 1661 to 1663. This simple redbrick house with green shutters is in Rijnsburg, near Leiden, where the oldest Dutch university was founded in 1575, and where Rembrandt and Jan Steen grew up. Spinoza rented a room there from the owner, Herman Homan, a medical man who specialized in painful early surgical techniques such as bloodletting.

The front of the house has a seventeenth-century plaque, applied after Spinoza had already moved away, which reads:

> Ah, if only people were wise and meant well
> the world would be a paradise,
> while now it is usually hell.

The house has been restored to something resembling what is must have been like when Spinoza lived there. Goose quills are neatly displayed on an ink stand. One can still see where Spinoza crafted his lenses for microscopes and telescopes. His library has been re-created with seventeenth-century copies of books he owned (the originals are lost, sadly). These include a Spanish edition of the Old Testament, books in Hebrew on religion and philosophy, scientific works in Latin, and some literature in Spanish, but not Dutch. There is also a guestbook. One of the signatures is from Albert Einstein, who visited the house in 1920.

The Rijnsburg house was made into a museum in 1897 and has been owned by the Spinoza House Society. The perspective on Spinoza in Rijnsburg was different from the one held by the society founded in The Hague. The view in Rijnsburg leaned toward science: Spinoza as a rationalist, who was convinced that the laws of nature should be studied with a rigorous logic. The "Hague School," in contrast, saw Spinoza as a great metaphysical thinker. They emphasized Spinoza's belief that the truth about nature and our place in it could in rare instances be intuited.

For many years before World War Two, the leading figure of the Domus Spinozana in The Hague was a legal scholar named Johan Carp. He was an ardent "Spinozist," who argued that Spinoza's idea of intuition as a route to knowledge was far more important than the philosopher's purported rationalism. Carp also had strong views on "organic democracy," with the law as an expression of popular feeling anchored in the national community. This developed into an ideal of the one-party state. Not surprisingly, Carp, a great admirer of the Jewish-born philosopher, became a keen member of the Dutch Nazi Party. Under German occupation, Carp rose to great heights. As secretary of state, he was responsible for the court that sent many resisters to their death. After the German defeat, Carp was sentenced to twelve years in prison.

What this squalid story shows is that Spinoza's complicated ideas are open to many interpretations. Seen by many people, Christians as well as Jews, as Satan's disciple during his lifetime, Spinoza has been regarded by many after his death as a saint. The question is, what kind of saint? A saint of rationalism or metaphysics, of atheism or pantheism, of liberalism or despotism, of Jewishness or antisemitism, as the father of democracy or totalitarianism? All these things have been said about Spinoza, some more plausibly than others. He was surely one of the pioneers of modern scientific thought. Albert Einstein said he believed in "Spinoza's God," but a Nazi could also claim the same man as the philosopher of spiritual fascist community. There is a Spinoza for everyone.[3]

The rediscovery of Spinoza, or "Spinozism," greatly agitated German intellectuals at the end of the eighteenth century, even as some French radicals claimed the Dutchman as one of their own—the atheist father of the French Revolution. Some Germans, Friedrich Heinrich Jacobi, for example, condemned him for the same reason, namely that Spinoza was an atheist, or at least that Spinoza's idea of God and nature being indivisible would inevitably result in atheism. But earlier in the century, Goethe saw Spinoza as an intellectual trailblazer, whose dispassionate attitude to God or nature inspired the German Enlightenment. Flaubert took a similar view, seeing Spinoza as an inspiration for scientifically observed naturalism.

In England, the Romantic poets Wordsworth, Coleridge, and Keats, with their exalted view of nature, worshipped Spinoza as well. Whether or not Spinoza had meant the same thing they did, the notion that man's emotions are determined by nature was something that they held sacred.

Heinrich Heine, a Jew who had converted to Lutheranism as an "entry ticket" to German society, adored Spinoza. He, too, like the English Romantics, had a pantheistic idea of nature, and the high-flown romantic language to match. Spinoza's philosophy, in Heine's words, was like "a forest of thoughts reaching to the sky, whose full-bloomed treetops sway while the sturdy tree trunks are rooted in the eternal soil." And Heine was not the only one to sanctify Spinoza in a peculiar way. The life of the man whom Heine liked to call "the little Dutch Jew" was "free of all blame, clean and unblemished, like that of his divine cousin, Jesus Christ. Like him, he suffered for his teachings. Like him, he wore the crown of thorns. Wherever a great spirit speaks his thoughts is Golgotha."[4]

It is hard to imagine this kind of imagery emerging from the mind of Karl Marx, who was just as obsessed with Spinoza as his friend Heine. What got him going was Spinoza's critique of religion: "The abolition of religion as the people's illusory happiness is the demand for their real happiness."[5] Marx wrote this. Spinoza and Ludwig Feuerbach inspired him. Feuerbach saw Spinoza as "the Moses of modern free-thinkers and materialists."[6] Marx read Spinoza's *Theological-Political Treatise* so carefully that he copied much of it from the original Latin as well as from the German translations. Marx's ideas on man's alienation from nature owed much to his reading of Spinoza, and so did his hopes for social change by exposing "false consciousness." To Marx, and other early socialists, Spinoza was the prophet of social transformation.

Then there was Sigmund Freud, another Spinozist, who saluted Spinoza as the man who sought salvation through self-knowledge. After clearing the rubble of myths, miracles, and destructive emotions, a way to scientific truth about ourselves would be found. Freud's Spinoza, one might say, was the inventor of modern psychology.

There are many other Spinozas too, a Dutch republican Spinoza, a Spanish aristocratic Spinoza, even a Zionist Spinoza. Spinoza wrote that Jews might one day found their own state once they had rid themselves of their religious prejudices. He did not specify where this state might be. But his statement had the approval of David Ben-Gurion, Israel's first prime minister.

I should come clean about my own interest in this extraordinary thinker. I am not an expert in philosophy and cannot presume to offer fresh insights into Spinoza's thinking. It would also be hard to improve on the excellent biography by Steven Nadler, whose book is about as exhaustive as one can be about a short life full of unknowns.[7] But when I was asked to write about Spinoza, my curiosity was piqued first because intellectual freedom has once again become an important issue, even in countries, such as the United States, that pride themselves on being uniquely free.

If one thing can be said unequivocally about Spinoza, it is that freedom of thought was his main preoccupation. Not only did he think that the best political order was one that protected the right to think and write in peace, but also that this very freedom would help to maintain such an order. He was an enemy of dogma, and particularly of dogmas based on beliefs and emotions rather than reasoned argument. To think freely was of course very dangerous in an age when religious dogma still dominated most people's lives. Spinoza wrote to a friend in 1665 about the "freedom of philosophizing and saying what we think." He wrote that he would "defend [this] in every way; here the preachers suppress it as much as they can with their excessive authority and aggressiveness."[8] He meant the Calvinists, or preachers of the Dutch Reformed Church who, in Spinoza's view, frightened the people into submission by spreading noxious superstitions. To thwart the authority of these preachers could be to risk one's life. Men died in prison for thinking the way Spinoza did.

Most of us no longer need to fear the preachers, even though evangelical zeal is far from dead, especially in parts of the United States. And few people in liberal democracies end up in prison for saying what they think. Yet liberal thinking is being challenged from many sides where ideologies are increasingly entrenched, by bigoted reactionaries as well as by progressives who believe there can be no deviation from their chosen paths to justice. Revisiting the life of a freethinker in the turbulent and contentious seventeenth century could help us come to grips with our own censorious time of dangerous political polarization.

Since most writing has an autobiographical element, I should declare my own. I was born and raised in the Netherlands, as was Spinoza. The history of his time, commonly known as the

SPINOZA

Dutch Golden Age, still weighed heavily on my education. Our sense of the past, instilled from an early age, was soaked in the mythology of two major conflicts: the eighty-year, mostly Protestant war against the Catholic Spanish king, which ended in Spinoza's lifetime, and the occupation by Nazi Germany. We were constantly reminded that our forebears died for our freedom and democracy. This was a cherished national myth, and it contained some truth. Even though Spinoza was not mentioned much, if at all, in my schooldays, some of his ideas about freedom, for which he was called the devil's disciple in his own time, were now considered to be part of our birthright. The seventeenth-century Dutch Republic is far removed from today's Netherlands, but I can recognize bits and pieces of it, an atmosphere, as it were, just as I can see a painting by Rembrandt, Potter, or Jan Steen with a certain degree of familiarity.

Many of Spinoza's closest friends were Mennonites. These men were not like the Mennonites in America, bearded figures in black hats and women in long dresses, descended mostly from rural Germans, who live traditional lives in secluded communities. The Dutch Mennonites were dissident Protestants with a strong liberal wing that rejected belief in the Holy Trinity and stressed the life of Christ, rather than his death, as a moral example. Like Catholics and Jews, they were tolerated in the seventeenth-century Dutch Republic, if they were discreet. Barred from public office and the guilds, many Mennonites went into business, and some became very wealthy, like the prominent Sephardic merchant families. Mennonites are still among the most liberal Protestants in the Netherlands today.

My paternal grandfather was a Mennonite minister with a skeptical mind and a strong aversion to religious or political dogmas. My father, not unusually for the son of a minister, was an atheist who regarded religion in much the same way as Spinoza did, as a form of superstition. My maternal grandfather was a Jew who had been raised in an orthodox home. By the time he married my secular Jewish grandmother, he had abandoned the customs and traditions of his youth. As a minister of the church, my Dutch grandfather must have believed in God. But his liberal views were similar to those of my Jewish grandfather. Religion was fine, so long as it made people behave decently and didn't foster intolerance. Neither grandfather would have called himself a Spinozist. But in many ways, they were not so far removed from him.

Spinoza was neither a Mennonite, nor in any religious sense a Jew. So how Jewish was his life? I have already indicated that he was commonly regarded as a Jew, despite his excommunication. This is still true, even in some unexpected places. His face adorns a poster on the wall of the bookstore in the Amsterdam Portuguese synagogue celebrating proud symbols of Dutch Jewish life, such as the Ajax soccer team, associated with "Jewish" Amsterdam, or what is left of it, and the novelist Arnon Grunberg, whose parents survived the Holocaust.

More serious attempts have been made to put Spinoza in a specifically Jewish light. Because of Spinoza's deep knowledge of other Jewish thinkers, notably the twelfth-century thinker Maimonides, he has been pressed by some scholars into a critical Jewish philosophical tradition. The Israeli scholar Yirmiyahu Yovel has portrayed Spinoza as a philosopher whose thinking was profoundly influenced by his Marrano family background. He believes that Spinoza's use of language and his "mastery of equivocation" were rooted in the habits of his ancestors who had to hide their faith behind a veil of Christian conversion in the face of the Iberian Inquisition.[9] Moses Hess, the nineteenth-century founder of left-wing Zionism, compared Spinoza to the ancient prophets—Spinoza as the Jewish prophet of messianic socialism.

Some of these claims might seem farfetched, even a bit zany. But there is, I think, an argument to be made that Spinoza did indeed lead a Jewish life, but it was a modern Jewish life. To Heine, Hess, Marx, Freud, and no doubt many others, Spinoza exemplified how to be Jewish without believing in Judaism. Being a secular Jew in Spinoza's time was a contradiction in terms; there could be no such thing. A communal identity was defined by religion. Given Spinoza's views on his ancestral religious beliefs, his rabbis had little choice but to excommunicate him. You could not reject Mosaic law and remain a Jew. Yet that is precisely what Heine, Hess, et al. wanted for themselves. Spinoza, at considerable personal cost, provided them with a model.

There is also another way to describe Spinoza's time on earth as being a Jewish life. Here Heine's idea of Spinoza as a Christ-like figure is less absurd than it may seem. One reason for Spinoza's deep distaste for religious institutions was his aversion to conflict; religious zealotry disturbed the social order that a philosopher needed to think in peace. But he was not content to be an armchair philosopher. His insistence on the use of human reason was an attempt to make his route to knowledge accessible to all people who wished to follow him, regardless of their culture, religion, or faith. He saw this as a quest for true happiness. He needed to understand nature (or God, which came down to the same thing) for his own happiness, but also to create a community in such a way as would allow others to achieve the same thing as easily and surely as possible.

Karl Marx was attempting something similar. His utopian vision of a classless society once "true communism" had been achieved was also a universal one. He, too, promised to deliver salvation of a secular kind. Which is perhaps why Marx and Spinoza (and perhaps Freud too) became such iconic figures, who were revered, even loved, in a way that other great philosophers were not. Kant, Hegel, and Hume were admired, but not loved. The only figure in the nonintellectual world who comes close is Napoleon, another outsider who offered liberty, equality, and fraternity to all, without necessarily delivering on his promise, and by exacting a price of horrendous bloodshed. He, too, is still revered in a way that other great military leaders are not, certainly not the duke of Wellington.

If everyone can be equal and free, then so can the Jews. In Marx's utopia, there would no longer be a "Jewish problem." Napoleon set much of Europe on fire, but he liberated the Jews from their Italian, French, and German ghettos and gave them equal rights. Spinoza had much to say about the Jews, not all of it friendly, but his ideal to diminish human strife by offering a universal path to God, truth, and self-knowledge would also set the Jews free. In that sense, if in no other, his was a great Jewish life.

2

————◆◆◆————

The Safe Place

SOME PEOPLE STILL REFER to the city of Amsterdam as Mokum, the Yiddish word for "place"—a place where one can feel safe. *Mokum* is one of many Yiddish words—*makker, goochem, ponem, mesjokke*—that are still commonly used in spoken Dutch long after more than 70 percent of Dutch Jews were murdered by the Nazis. Before 1940, up to eighty thousand Jews lived in Amsterdam. Only about five thousand survived.

Amsterdam was not the only city with this Yiddish name; Berlin had it too, as well as several other cities in the Netherlands, such as Delft and Alkmaar. But Amsterdam is the only place to which the name stuck. What is left of Jewish Amsterdam is mostly folklore now. Supporters of Ajax, the main Amsterdam soccer club, like to call themselves the "Super Jews" and brandish Israeli flags, much to the irritation of the club's officials, who tried to ban the practice as needlessly provocative. The supporters started doing this in reaction to fans from clubs in

Rotterdam, Utrecht, or The Hague, who found it amusing to identify the Amsterdammers as "the Yids" (or worse names), even though any real connection to Jews was lost long ago.

The idea of Amsterdam as a safe place for Jews began at the beginning of the seventeenth century, a time when Jews were still barred from England, persecuted in Spain and Portugal, and forced to live in ghettos in Germany and Italy. The Republic of the United Netherlands was less a nation-state than a confederation of seven mostly Protestant provinces, united in rebellion against the Catholic king of Spain—the war that lasted eighty years, until 1648. Holland was the largest of the seven provinces, and Amsterdam the biggest city in Holland.

Since the fourteenth century, Jews in Spain were forced to convert to avoid persecution, or after 1492, being expelled. This was enforced by the infamous Inquisition. They were the "Conversos" or "Marranos." Some only pretended to convert but stuck to their own faith in secret as "crypto-Jews." But conversion was often not enough. Racial laws made life for people with Jewish or Muslim roots impossible. Many fled to Portugal to escape the Spanish Inquisition. Soon, the Portuguese Inquisition was even more ferocious than the Spanish. Many Marranos and crypto-Jews drifted to northern cities, such as Antwerp in the Catholic Southern Netherlands, where they were classified as Portuguese. While the Dutch Republic was at war with Spain, it was safer to be called Portuguese. The phrase "Portuguese trader" was almost synonymous with Jews of one kind or another. When Spanish military campaigns and economic blockades isolated Antwerp from the Northern Netherlands at the end of the sixteenth century, its position as a major international hub of commerce was lost, and many "Portuguese" moved farther north, to the Dutch Republic that had declared its independence from the Spanish crown in 1581.

With their commercial know-how and international connections, the Portuguese were mostly welcomed in Dutch cities.

Anybody or anything was generally welcomed by the Dutch if it was good for business. (The Dutch were even happy to do business on the sly with Spain, which could be quite profitable.) And besides, when the seven provinces of the Dutch Republic united in 1579, the so-called Union of Utrecht decreed that its citizens could practice their religions without question. Voltaire's description of the eighteenth-century London Stock Exchange, where Christians, Jews, and Muslims traded freely as though they were of the same faith and only applied the word *infidel* to people who went bankrupt, would fit the Republic of the United Netherlands quite nicely.

The link between free trade and freedom was even the basis of a well-known political theory developed by two brothers, Pieter and Johan de la Court, whom Spinoza might have known personally, and certainly read carefully. They were among the great pioneers of what Jonathan Israel calls the Radical Enlightenment.[1] They wrote in their *Political Discourses* (Politike discoursen), published in 1662: "Commerce is not tied to any one place. People will thrive wherever merchants are least hindered and given most freedom to make and conserve their profits."[2]

Here is Spinoza himself about his native city, Amsterdam, which "knows by experience the fruits of this liberty." In this "most outstanding city," he writes, with a degree of polemical exaggeration, when people "entrust their goods to someone, the only thing they care to know is whether the person is rich or poor, and whether he usually acts in good faith or not."[3]

This was the ideal anyway, a remarkable ideal in the sixteenth and seventeenth centuries, but things were not quite so simple. In the beginning, Portuguese were welcomed as Christians in the Dutch Republic, and not as Jews. The first attempts to use Dutch freedoms to revive the religious practices and traditions of their Sephardic ancestors only began in the first decade of the next century. The first Jewish congregations met in private homes until 1614, when a warehouse was rented for these purposes.

There are some legendary founding fathers of the Dutch Sephardim, officially known as the Portuguese Nation. A certain Moses Uriel Halevy, who spoke neither Spanish nor Portuguese, but had the skills of circumcision and kosher butchery, settled in Amsterdam in 1603 and discreetly started a new Jewish community. He was an Ashkenazic Jew, originally from Germany, but most of the Portuguese knew so little about Judaism that they were happy to learn from a German rabbi. Alas, he was not quite discreet enough. Suspicious Calvinists mistook Hebrew prayers for a kind of Latin, and arrested Halevy on suspicion that he was a Catholic. (An alternative account suggests that he was suspected of fencing stolen goods.) A man named Jacob Tirado persuaded the authorities that Halevy and his small congregation were Jews, and that Jews were good for business. Halevy was released. But the Dutch weren't sure what to do with the influx of all these Portuguese who were now claiming to be Jews.

The first decade of the seventeenth century, when these events took place, was a relatively liberal period when the cosmopolitan statesman Johan van Oldenbarnevelt was in power, and the great jurist Hugo Grotius was one of his legal officials. Grotius was a member of the committee asked to advise on what was to be done about the Portuguese. He believed, upon careful consideration, that Jews should be allowed to conduct their business in the republic as free men: "Plainly God desires them to live somewhere. Why then not here rather than elsewhere?" Even though the Amsterdam Jews' knowledge of Hebrew might have been patchy at best, Grotius assumed this might be useful to pious Christians. But even the free-spirited Grotius needed to protect the Dutch Reformed Church and made it clear that the republic should not tolerate "atheists or impious people," whatever their stated religion.[4]

The States General, the central legislative organ of the republic, decided in the end that each city and town should make its own rules on Jewish settlement. Amsterdam was less open at first than some other places, such as Haarlem. But the upshot was that Jews could practice their religion, so long as it didn't clash with Calvinism on such vital matters as the immortality of the soul, belief in the afterlife, God the creator, or the divine origins of the Holy Scripture—all dogmas that Spinoza would later repudiate, with dramatic effect. Orthodoxy was imposed by the Calvinist preachers as much as by the rabbis brought to the republic from places such as Venice or Constantinople, to teach the Marranos and lapsed Jews how to revive their traditions.

There were other restrictions on Jews. Even though they were never forced to live in ghettos, nor wear any distinctive dress—pointed hats and the like—they were forbidden from having sexual relations with gentiles, and like Catholics and Protestant dissidents, they could not join the guilds. The relative status of Catholics in seventeenth-century Amsterdam can still be gauged by visiting one of their tiny hidden chapels, where Catholics had to keep their heads down, as it were, even as the Sephardim were allowed to build the gigantic Portuguese synagogue that still stands as one of the city's great landmarks.

One person who might have fallen foul of the rules governing Jewish life was Spinoza's great-uncle Abraham de Spinoza, a respected member of Beth Chaim, the first Portuguese synagogue in Amsterdam. He was arrested for having had improper relations with his gentile maidservant, named Toboda Ockema. This type of domestic arrangement was not uncommon. But Jews were quickly suspected by straightlaced Protestants of being especially lecherous. The famous historian of Jewish life in Amsterdam A. M. Vaz Dias reminds his readers why. After all, "among the Israelites who had come from the south there was a different set of moral values than among the strict Calvinists."[5]

A degree of tolerance, as Voltaire observed, is often a mark of business-minded societies. The Dutch have long vaunted their tolerance as a vital element of their national self-regard. One word for tolerance in Dutch is *gedogen*, meaning to turn a blind eye to something that is not strictly legal, and possibly undesirable, but worth putting up with, especially when there is money to be made. In modern times, for example, Dutch governments have had a *gedoogbeleid*, or policy of tolerance, toward prostitution, until it was legalized in 2000, and the sale of soft drugs, which is still illegal, but widely practiced—the *use* of soft drugs is not illegal. That the policy of *gedogen* turned Amsterdam into a center of organized crime, with gangs dealing in hard as well as soft drugs and trafficking in women, was an unintended consequence.

But *gedogen* was indisputably good for the Jews of the seventeenth century and after. Full civil rights for Jews only came after the invasion of the Netherlands by the French army in 1795. All citizens became equal under French law. Until then, however, life had been better for many Jews in Amsterdam than in most places in Europe. Mokum had earned its name. But the tolerant society was not invulnerable to intolerant currents running through the Dutch Republic.

A few decades before Spinoza was born, the republic was wracked by a battle of theologians that became fiercely political, with fatal consequences for some of the most liberal leaders. It all began with a dispute between a professor of theology named Jacobus Arminius and a Flemish theologian named Franciscus Gomarus. Arminius, although a Dutch Reformed pastor himself, challenged Calvin's ideas on grace and predestination. He didn't believe that people were destined to go to heaven or hell regardless of their personal behavior. A person could find salvation through his or her own efforts. And matters of conscience should be left to individuals. The relatively liberal-minded Arminius had been inspired by others before him, such as Dirck

Coornhert, who had advocated religious tolerance and didn't believe that heretics should be executed.

Gomarus denounced Arminius and his followers as dangerous heretics, even papists. The Arminians became known as the Remonstrants after 1610, when they remonstrated for religious tolerance. Oldenbarnevelt was on the side of the Remonstrants. Prince Maurits of Orange, the "stadtholder," in effect the aristocratic head of state and military commander-in-chief, sided with the Counter-Remonstrants—out of opportunism more than conviction. What started as a professorial quarrel about predestination became a political fight over foreign policy, how to carry on with the war against Spain, and such domestic issues as the division of authority between church, state, stadtholder, and States General. Oldenbarnevelt, fearing a military coup, tried to curtail the powers of Prince Maurits. The conservatives won in the end. A synod convened in Dordrecht in 1619 decided that the Remonstrants should be expelled from the Dutch Reformed Church; Grotius was locked up in prison; and Oldenbarnevelt was publicly beheaded in The Hague. Gomarus, perhaps not so incidentally, also wanted more restrictions to be placed on the Jews.

How to treat people outside the Calvinist faith was in fact a fiercely contested issue. Since the Reformed Church was the official religion of the Dutch Republic, it was up to the state to protect its citizens from "false religions." This included Catholics and Jews. Some strict theologians were in favor of banning them. But in this instance, the policy of *gedogen* was applied. Mostly, so long as non-Calvinists did not threaten the social order, they could be tolerated.

This meant that the budding Sephardic community in Amsterdam had to be very careful not to do anything to rile the Calvinists. The rabbis had to make sure that Jewish doubters and freethinkers, who were drawn to philosophical ideas more than divine revelations in the Bible, did not make trouble. This was not always a simple matter. One prominent rabbi in Spinoza's synagogue was Menasseh ben Israel, from a Portuguese Marrano family. He was the man who tried to persuade Oliver Cromwell to allow Jews to settle in England. Menasseh was also a successful printer and publisher of religious books in many languages, which found an eager clientele among Jews and Christians all over Europe. His most famous work was *The Conciliator* (El conciliador), only completed in the 1650s, which aimed to teach relatively ignorant Marranos about their ancestral faith without annoying the Christians. While clearing up apparent inconsistencies in the sacred texts, the rabbi carefully defended orthodox Judaism. And yet, on the question of predestination, he was with the Arminians. He had corresponded with Grotius and other liberal thinkers. Rembrandt did an etching of someone who may have been Menasseh, whom Rembrandt knew. All this made him enemies inside the Jewish community. He always felt he didn't get the respect he deserved. More conservative rabbis were often placed above him in the religious hierarchy. If Christians had to be cautious about what they said in public, Jews had to be even more so.

Although Jews were never forced to live in ghettos, there is a part of Amsterdam where many of them lived since the seventeenth century. You can still tell where it is by the almost complete absence of any buildings built before the 1980s, which is unique in the old center of a city of narrow gabled houses, many of which are centuries old. The opera house and the town hall, both built in the 1980s, stand in the middle of an area that was once an island reclaimed from the Amstel that gave the city its name. This district used to be called Vlooienburg, *vlooi* being an old Dutch word for "flood." Next to the town hall is a much-reduced version of what was once a bustling flea market.

The Portuguese synagogue, or Snoge, finished in 1675, still looms over the area, opposite the much lower former Ashkenazi synagogue, now the Jewish Museum.

The reason why almost everything is relatively new (and often ugly) in the area is painful. Jews from all over the country were forced to live there by the Nazis during the German occupation, creating a ghetto for the first time. By 1943 most of them had been deported to the death camps, and the houses where they had lived in terror of constant raids were abandoned. During the freezing winter of 1944, people stripped these dwellings of wood and furniture for fuel. After the war, the ruined houses were left to rot for decades before they were torn down for redevelopment and a new subway line.

Various monuments to the Holocaust dot the streets around the synagogues and town hall. The first memorial to the murdered Jews was a strange one, built in 1950 as a "monument of Jewish gratitude" for the "protective love" of Dutch helpers and resisters. There indeed had been some resistance and some helpers, but the monument, designed by a Holocaust survivor, was still an embarrassing piece of whitewashing. A monument sculpted from broken mirrors was placed in a nearby park in 1970 to remember the people murdered in Auschwitz. In 2020 a long, zigzagging brick wall was put up with the names of 102,000 Jews (and 220 Sinti and Roma) deported to the death camps. Very near there, on the corner of what was once the Vlooienburg island, stands Spinoza, decorated with exotic birds on his long bronze cloak as symbols of the city's diverse population. The statue stands within sight of his birthplace but is shielded from the Portuguese synagogue, to avoid unpleasant associations. Below Spinoza's feet are his words engraved in granite: "The aim of the state is freedom."

Vlooienburg was neither the most prosperous part of seventeenth-century Amsterdam, nor by any means the poorest.

Trade in timber and art were the main businesses. The street where Spinoza was born was called Houtgracht, meaning "Lumber Canal." Art was both made and sold in the area. Rembrandt lived on the edge of Vlooienburg. His grand, three-story house on the Jodenbreestraat (Jewish Broadway) is one of the few old buildings left. Some of the local Jews found their way into his biblical paintings as models. A wealthy Jew named Daniel Pinto was Rembrandt's neighbor. Saul Levi Morteira, the intransigent rabbi who would be Spinoza's nemesis, lived on the other side of the street. Paulus Potter, the painter of cows, lived around the corner for a time.

Some members of the Portuguese Nation quickly became very rich. Especially in times when the war against Spain was in a lull—there was a welcome truce between 1609 and 1621—contacts in Spain and Portugal, as well as in the South American colonies, enabled Jewish merchants to do a brisk trade in wine, olive oil, dry fruits, anchovies, spices, Spanish linen, and other desirable goods from warmer countries. From Amsterdam, they traded with cities with large Jewish populations such as Hamburg and Livorno. Some of the merchants sailed rather close to the wind, buying and selling pirated goods from North Africa, or shipping arms to Spain, the enemy of the republic and the scourge of the Jews. Jewish traders often disguised their identities by adopting Dutch names. Dutch colonial expansion, and the ruthless monopolies of the Dutch East India Company, offered further opportunities. Jews traded silk from China, slaves from Africa, diamonds from India, as well as tobacco and sugar from the plantations in South America, where crypto-Jews and Marranos often owned their own slaves. The sugar trade was dominated by the Amsterdam Sephardim, much to the annoyance of their gentile rivals. Even though the richest gentiles in Amsterdam were much richer than the richest Jews, the most successful Portuguese merchants were not shy about showing off their wealth. They lived lives of great opulence. Some of the finest country houses with French gardens along the Vecht River outside Amsterdam once belonged to them.

A few grandees also found an entrée into Dutch high society. Diego Duarte was a banker and jeweler based in Antwerp. His collection of paintings by Rubens, Holbein, Titian, and Raphael was famous. He was a friend of Constantijn Huygens, the poet, composer, and secretary to the princes of Orange. Huygens's son, the scientist Christiaan Huygens, would one day befriend Spinoza, "the Jew of Voorburg." Duarte's daughter, Francisca, settled in Holland, became a member of Huygens's artistic circle, and sang for the exiled Maria de Medici, who had once been queen of France.

You can pick up something of the tone of the Sephardic upper class of Amsterdam on the spot where many of them are buried. One of the irksome regulations still governing Jewish life was the refusal of municipal authorities to let Jews bury their dead inside the city—irksome since, according to the Jewish law, Jews need to be buried quickly. The bodies had to be transported in boats along the Amstel River to a pretty little village named Ouderkerk. Beth Haim, the Portuguese Jewish cemetery, beautifully painted in the 1650s by Jacob van Ruisdael, is still there in all its faded splendor. There they all lie: Rabbi Menasseh; Samuel Palache, the Moroccan diplomat; the Italian rabbi Joseph Pardo; Eliahu Montalto, personal physician to Maria de Medici; Miguel (Michael) and Hanna Deborah Spinoza, Baruch's parents; and Isaac, his grandfather. The egg-white tombstones, described by an English visitor in 1641 as "very stately of cost," are beautifully carved with letters in Hebrew, Spanish, and Portuguese, as well as grand family crests and scenes from the Bible: Jacob dreaming, David strumming his lyre, Moses holding up the tablets, Mordechai on his horse, and so on.[6] The impression is one of Spanish grandeur, and to some conservative Jewish eyes this would be an affront to the second commandment against graven images. The Israeli Spinoza scholar Yirmiyahu Yovel is right when he says that a visitor might feel one "has entered a baroque cemetery of the aristocracy or upper bourgeoisie in one of the catholic states of southern Europe."[7]

I received precisely the same impression when I was shown seventeenth-century Jewish books, printed in Amsterdam, at the Ets Haim library of the Portuguese synagogue in Amsterdam: finely crafted illustrations are often copied from Christian books with minor alterations. The Ouderkerk tombs show how strong Christian influence was on the recently Judaized former Marranos. That, and a deep attachment to the culture of a country from which they had been expelled, often after great savagery. The Spanish affectations of seventeenth-century Sephardim in Amsterdam might be compared to the unshakable conviction of persecuted German Jews in the twentieth century that German *Kultur* was still superior to all else. The poet Daniel Levi de Barrios (pen name Miguel de Barrios) wrote about his coreligionists that they were "generally so haughty that even the poorest would not condescend to serve the rich, since he would regard himself as just as noble."[8] The fine manners of the Spanish gentry were evident even in Spinoza's demeanor, although he had no aspirations toward any kind of high life or grandiosity. His literary taste would always remain Spanish.

The superior attitudes of the Dutch Sephardim never completely vanished. I grew up with people called Vas Nunes or Mendes de Leon. They were no less snobbish than gentiles of their class in The Hague, and the gentiles could be very snobbish indeed. Hispanic disdain for lesser breeds showed itself in the way seventeenth-century Portuguese regarded and treated the Ashkenazim.

Pogroms and the horrors of the Thirty Years' War (1618–48), which ravaged much of the German lands, drove many Ashkenazim to the promised city of Amsterdam. Most were penniless, filthy, dressed in rags, and had to beg to stay alive. To the Portuguese Nation, they were a deep embarrassment. Money was collected to help the most indigent, to be sure, but the Sephardim were happy to assist the city authorities in their efforts to push these Yiddish-speaking *"schnorrer"* back to where they came from. Some managed to hang on in Amsterdam nonetheless, working as moneylenders, petty traders, or servants to Sephardic Jews. Servants could not break their contracts without official approval of the nation's authorities. *Tudesca*, literally meaning "German," was another word for "servant." Ashkenazim were not allowed to enter the Portuguese synagogue. Even though the Portuguese had had to enlist several Ashkenazic rabbis, including Saul Levi Morteira, to teach them in the old traditions, the Ashkenazim were accused of "distorting" the Jewish faith.

These prejudices have had a long life. Isaac de Pinto was a learned Dutch philosopher in the eighteenth century with enlightened ideas who actively campaigned for Jewish emancipation. He wrote mainly in French and Spanish. A major investor in the Dutch East India Company, De Pinto became the company's president in 1750, in which capacity he was visited by Frederick the Great. His grand house still stands on the Herengracht in Amsterdam with the proud family crest prominently displayed, and the even bigger house where he was born is one of the very few buildings in the old Jewish quarter to have survived the war. This Sephardic grandee was much disturbed by Voltaire's notorious attacks on Jews and their faith. He wrote a strong riposte in 1762, entitled *Apology for the Jewish Nation, or Critical Reflections* (Apologie pour la nation Juive, ou réflexions critiques). Voltaire was making a big mistake, De Pinto argued, by associating or confusing Ashkenazim with Sephardim. Any Portuguese Jew who married an Ashkenazic Jew would no longer be regarded as a member of the Portuguese synagogue. Such a match would be seen as a betrayal of his noble tribe. As Henry

Méchoulan, from whose book I have quoted these words, quite rightly remarks: "If such prejudices could be defended in the age of Enlightenment, they must have been a great deal fiercer in the century before."[9]

3

Born to Strife

SUCH THEN WAS THE WORLD into which Baruch Spinoza was born on November 24, 1632. Amsterdam was a safe place for Portuguese Sephardim in a country still riven by conflicts, religious and political, which often came down to the same thing. He was named Baruch after his maternal grandfather, a Portuguese merchant. His paternal family, the d'Espinozas, or Despinozas, as they were still called, had arrived in Holland from France in the 1620s, after leaving Portugal, where Michael, Spinoza's father, was born. Michael's uncle Abraham and his father, Isaac, had settled in Rotterdam. Hanna Deborah, Spinoza's mother, was Michael's second wife.

Baruch, known to family and friends as Bento, was the second d'Espinoza, after his elder brother Isaac, in many generations to be born as a Jew, and not a crypto-Jew. It has been argued, most famously by Yirmiyahu Yovel, that Spinoza's Marrano family background marked his thinking in some profound way.

28

In Yovel's opinion, "Spinoza's mastery of equivocation and dual language brings to a climax devices and sensibilities in which the Marranos had excelled for generations."[1] Perhaps. But this is hard to prove. Double-talk is an accusation often leveled at unpopular religious minorities, first the Jews, later Muslims. Forcing people to convert or conform can result in precisely the kind of defensive behavior that confirms the prejudices of the majority. Spinoza, at any rate, always regarded himself as a loyal citizen of the Dutch Republic, where he spent all his life without setting foot elsewhere. But he was most comfortable speaking in Portuguese, the family language of his childhood. He was also fluent in Spanish and Hebrew, which he learned at school. Later he acquired good but not exactly stylish Latin. His Dutch was functional, but never more than that, which embarrassed him.

Spinoza's childhood home on Vlooienburg, amid lumberyards, artists' studios, and synagogues discreetly tucked away in private houses, was comfortable, reflecting the social status of Michael, who was a prosperous but not enormously rich merchant. The house no longer exists, alas. On its spot stands the Moses and Aaron Church, once a semi-clandestine place of worship for Amsterdam's Catholics. Michael's main business was in Mediterranean goods from Spain and North Africa—dried fruits, olive oil, and the like. Trade also went in the opposite direction, even though exporting goods to Spain, still the archenemy, not just of the Dutch Republic, but of the persecuted Jews, was not officially allowed. Nonetheless, ships sailing under false flags made their way from Holland to Lisbon or Málaga. Michael was clearly well-connected with businessmen all over Europe. One of his associates was Antonio Fernandez Carvajal, a crypto-Jew in London who would go on to establish the first synagogue there.

Jewish merchants, such as Michael d'Espinoza, were always vulnerable to political events. They thrived during the truce between Spain and the Dutch Republic from 1609 and 1621, but war, not just with Spain but several times with England too, was bad for business, except perhaps for arms traders. The sugar trade benefitted greatly from Dutch possessions in Brazil, but when Portugal took over the colony, the slave plantations changed hands, and this line of business collapsed. Cargo was sometimes lost at sea because of piracy, storms, or attacks from foreign powers. This happened on several occasions to Michael, who had the added misfortune of taking on the debts of others that he couldn't repay.

That Michael was even asked to guarantee other people's debts shows that he was a man of substance in the Jewish community of Amsterdam. He had a seat among the *parnassim*, the lay directors who took care of taxes, poor relief, and other communal obligations. Since they couldn't afford any friction with the Calvinist authorities, this board of Jewish notables was necessarily conservative. Michael would have been one of the Sephardic officials who had to deal with the noisome presence of Ashkenazic mendicants. They also had to make sure that Jewish worship and celebrations would be kept discreet enough not to annoy the Christians, who were always easy to annoy, and that kosher butchery and other important religious matters were kept in the hands of respectable people, who were naturally Sephardim.

Never a robust woman, Spinoza's mother, Hanna Deborah, died of consumption in 1638, when he was only five. A delicate figure himself, with a pale, slender face, thick black eyebrows, and dark, hooded eyes, Spinoza may well have inherited her fragile condition. He had an older sister, Miriam, an older brother, Isaac, who died young, and a younger brother, Gabriel. Then there was another sister, Rebecca, who was probably Hanna's daughter, even though some have claimed that she was a child of Michael's third wife, Esther. Things cannot have been easy for the family when Spinoza started school at the Talmud Torah a year after his mother's death. The young pupils were instructed in Spanish, as well as Hebrew, a language most of their Marrano parents would not have known, apart from muttering a few set phrases in the synagogue. Different rabbis taught them to read the Five Books of Moses, the Torah, and other sacred texts. The highest class was taught Talmud by Rabbi Morteira.

The level of Spinoza's early schooling was evidently quite high. Steven Nadler, Spinoza's biographer, quotes a visitor from Poland named Shabetthai Bass, who recalled seeing "tender children as small as grasshoppers. . . . In my eyes they were like prodigies because of their unusual familiarity with the entire Bible and with the science of grammar. They possessed the ability to compose verses and poems and to speak a pure Hebrew. Happy the eye that has seen all these things."[2]

Some of Spinoza's schoolmates at Talmud Torah went on to have extraordinary careers that diverged widely from his own. One dreamy boy from a prominent Marrano family, named Moses ben Mordecai Zacuto, had a strong mystical bent. He learned Latin as a schoolboy, but later immersed himself in the esoteric codes of the Kabbalah and was so ashamed of learning Latin that he fasted for forty days to forget that profane language. Zacuto ended up as a rabbi in Italy. Another religious romantic among Spinoza's classmates was Isaac Naar, born in Hamburg to Marrano parents. He, too, grew up to become an Italian rabbi, after falling under the spell of Sabbatai Tzvi, the Jewish mystic from Smyrna who claimed to be the long-awaited messiah in 1648. Many Sephardim in Amsterdam became devotees of Sabbatai in the 1660s. Candles were lit all over Vlooienburg to celebrate his miraculous coming. Contrary to their normal habit of keeping their heads down in public, Jews thronged the streets singing and dancing with joy. Some worshippers sold all their belongings to pay for a one-way trip to Palestine, where they hoped to meet the savior. So many Jews were boarding ships bound for the Holy Land that the city authorities worried about the damage a Jewish exodus might do to business. This eruption of religious hysteria finally calmed down after the false messiah was arrested in Constantinople by the Ottoman imperial authorities in 1666. Rather than submitting to a death sentence, he chose to convert to Islam. The sincerity of his conversion might be questioned, since Sabbatai was discovered singing psalms with Jews in Constantinople. He, too, might have spent years of his life dissembling. Expelled from the Ottoman capital, he died alone and poor in a pirates' den on the Adriatic coast. His memory is kept alive by a small Turkish sect called the Dönme, who are nominally Muslim, but still dabble in Jewish mysticism. Like so many sects, these diehard followers of the messiah ended up splitting into different factions that wanted to have nothing to do with each other.

All this took place long after Spinoza had left school. His youth would have been spent in an entirely Sephardic milieu, where people dressed like respectable Dutch burghers in black silk and white ruffs and retained the airs of Spanish aristocrats. He could walk to the Talmud Torah school and the synagogue, which were just minutes from his home. Since life was conducted in Portuguese, he might as well have been living in Porto or Lisbon, minus the religious persecution, of course. But Spinoza would have seen plenty of Dutch gentiles, possibly including Rembrandt himself, enjoying a stroll around the neighborhood. Gentiles even came to the Portuguese synagogue out of curiosity, or to hear well-known rabbis preach—Menasseh was popular among non-Jews. One of the men who frequented the synagogue was an eccentric figure named Jan Pietersz, also known as Beelthouwer, meaning "Sculptor."

Born around 1603, the Sculptor was a poet, schoolmaster, and spiritual caretaker for sick people. His poems were clumsy, but Jan Pietersz had an original mind. He taught himself Hebrew and took a benevolent view of the Jews, whom he tried to convince, without conspicuous success, that Jesus was the true

son of God. He would turn up at the synagogue to argue with
Rabbi Morteira, among others, pointing out their faulty interpretations of the sacred texts. This might not have endeared him
to Morteira, who probably found him a bore, and according to
Dutch law would have been prohibited from arguing religious
affairs with him anyway. But the Sculptor irritated the Calvinists much more by doubting the Holy Trinity and rejecting Calvinist views on predestination. God's grace, he believed, could
surely save the souls of Jews and other infidels if they were
good people. For this, he was accused of Socinianism, the non-
trinitarian heterodoxy preached by Faustus Socinus in the sixteenth century. Socinianists were dangerous heretics in Dutch
Reformed eyes since they didn't believe in God's omniscience
or the doctrine of original sin. Whether or not the Sculptor
really was a Socinianist, he was duly excommunicated from his
church, expelled from Dordrecht, his hometown, and "delivered to Satan," in the words of his local preacher.[3] Beelthouwer
was not without wit, however, for some years later he denounced
this minister as a false prophet, since Satan had not yet embraced
him in any shape or form. In time, he took up notions of God's
immanence in nature that were close to Spinoza's philosophy.

There is no proof that Spinoza ever saw this interesting
man in action, but he would have been aware from an early age
of dissenting views on religious doctrine, and the fierce reactions they invariably provoked. There had been serious disputes
inside the Portuguese community that mirrored the splits among
Calvin's followers, though not necessarily for the same reasons.
At the time of Spinoza's birth, there were three synagogues to
serve the spiritual needs of the Portuguese Nation: Beth Jacob,
Nave Shalom, and Beth Israel. To paper over their frequent quarrels, they finally merged in 1639. The most serious conflict was
between the very young Rabbi Isaac Aboab de Fonseca, who
was born to a Marrano family in Portugal, and the older Rabbi
Morteira. Aboab was a kabbalist with a strong taste for mysti-

cism. Morteira was a more conservative religious scholar. The matter of dispute was an important one to Marranos and former Marranos: Was a Jew who converted to the Christian faith still a Jew? If not, his soul would be damned. Aboab couldn't accept this. Surely, even Jews who had converted could find a place in the world-to-come. Morteira totally disagreed. Those who did not live as Jews were traitors who could no longer be part of the community, now or in the afterlife. He thought that "it was blasphemy to believe that these extremely wicked people have not been given an eternal punishment."[4] Like many immigrants, always and in all places, the Jews of Amsterdam were defensive about their communal identity, particularly because most of them, like Aboab himself, had been nominal Christians so recently and still had relatives on the Iberian peninsula.

The issue became too heated and complex for the local rabbis to solve, so it went to the rabbinic court in Venice, which tried to persuade Aboab to renounce his views. When he refused, the Venice rabbis sided with Morteira. Deciding that life in Amsterdam had become impossible, Aboab later moved to South America, where he became a rabbi in Recife, a part of Brazil then still held by the Dutch; many of the Dutch colonizers were in fact Portuguese Jews. When the Dutch lost their colony to Portugal in 1654, and the Inquisition threatened the Jews once more, Aboab returned to Amsterdam. Two years later he would preside over Spinoza's banishment from the synagogue. His colleague at the time of this fearsome act was none other than his old adversary, Rabbi Saul Levi Morteira.

Not much is known about Spinoza as a young schoolboy. Although he may not have completed all six grades of his school, and the story that Michael wanted his son to be a rabbi is open to doubt, Spinoza was a good enough student to attend yeshiva, possibly under Rabbi Morteira, where he acquired sufficient knowledge to become a daring critic of biblical texts and, near the end of his life, the author of a book on Hebrew grammar.

Most of what we can surmise about his childhood comes from well-polished anecdotes that may or may not be true. Some of these stories suggest, perhaps by design, that he was not just a bookish stranger to worldly affairs, a *Luftmensch*. When he was only ten, Spinoza was sent by his father to pick up some money owed by an old lady. Michael had taught his son to be vigilant and never to be fooled by false piety. The errand was to be a test of Spinoza's wits. The old woman asked the boy to wait while she finished her prayers. After praising Spinoza's father for his religious devotion, she quickly tried to fumble some cash into the child's bag. Sensing that there was something not quite right, Spinoza insisted on counting the money despite the lady's protests. She had indeed shortchanged him by slipping a few ducats through a gap in the table.

Since Spinoza clearly was not a *Luftmensch*, he would have been sharply aware of the religious strife shaking up society outside his narrow circle as well. Among the Protestants, the contentions between orthodox Calvinists and relatively liberal Remonstrants going back to the arguments between Gomarus and Arminius continued. And so did the political interests that attached themselves to these conflicting parties. Followers of the House of Orange, with its hereditary stadtholders, took the side of the Counter-Remonstrants. The "Orangists," most powerful in the rural provinces outside Holland, were more martial and authoritarian than the men from prominent merchant families who governed as so-called regents in municipal councils and the States General, the confederate legislative chamber. These patrician regents, beautifully painted by Frans Hals in their sober but expensive black finery, were not democrats by any means. But they were liberal compared to the Orangists. For much of the seventeenth century, regents and the stadtholders battled for power in the Dutch Republic. The difference was essentially between aristocratic authority, supported by the Reformed Church, and an enlightened oligarchy of an urban-based, business-minded elite. The regents were at the peak of their powers between 1650 and 1672, when they had managed to get rid of stadtholders altogether. This was the heart of the much-celebrated Dutch Golden Age of Rembrandt, Vermeer, the playwright Joost van den Vondel, and the great liberal statesmen Johan and Cornelis de Witt. But when Spinoza was growing up, Prince Frederik Hendrik, son of William the Silent, and his Calvinist faction still held sway. Paintings of Frederik Hendrik, the great warrior prince, show a large, swaggering figure, usually dressed in suits of armor. Even though Spinoza's ideals were democratic, he was always aware that his life as a freethinker was safer under the oligarchic regents, many of whom read his books, than under the Orangists, whom he despised.

Some of the most divisive issues in the mid-seventeenth century would have put the Amsterdam Sephardim in a tight spot, which is precisely where they didn't want to be. Whether or not to continue the war against Spain was one such issue. The regents, whose instincts were more commercial than war-like, looked for ways to end the war, even if that meant making concessions to the Catholics living mostly in the southern provinces of the Dutch Republic. Such concessions were unacceptable to the Calvinists, who found papists almost as abominable as Jews. And Frederik Hendrik, as commander of the army and navy, was all for war, in the hope of adding to his already considerable military victories and boosting his own position in the republic. Peace would obviously have been better for the Amsterdam Jews, who had done so well out of trade with Spain. But they had to be careful, as always, not to upset any establishment, and certainly not the House of Orange.

Frederik Hendrik was not, however, unmindful of his own financial considerations. On at least one occasion this involved the Amsterdam Jews. In 1642, when King Charles I of England was being challenged by his parliamentary enemies and civil war was brewing, his consort, the Catholic Queen Henrietta Maria, traveled to Holland with their daughter, Mary. Mary, who was the same age as Spinoza, came to marry Frederik Hendrik's son, William, who was only fifteen at the time, five years older than his bride. The stadtholder could do with royal support. Both he and Charles were fighting for aristocratic privileges. A match between the two children was meant to warm their relations and further their cause. Queen Henrietta, who was suffering from a bad cold and a toothache, was also on a mission to raise money for her husband's side in the struggle against the English and Scottish parliaments. She hoped to use some of the crown jewels as collateral for a substantial loan and to sell other precious heirlooms. Most potential buyers tended to shy away from such a transaction, however, fearing political trouble. And so, in desperation, the queen's people turned to the Jews of Amsterdam, who agreed to a loan if Frederik Hendrik would guarantee it.

On May 22, 1642, the Portuguese synagogue was visited by the august royal delegation, led by Frederik Hendrik and Queen Henrietta, who had expressed her wish to see the Jews at prayer. They were greeted by the *parnassim*, with Michael d'Espinoza no doubt in attendance. Rabbi Menasseh had the honor of welcoming the illustrious visitors. This was an important political event for the Jews as well. The rabbi indicated why, saying:

> We no longer look upon Castille and Portugal, but upon Holland as our fatherland. We no longer wait upon the Spanish or Portuguese King, but upon Their Excellencies the States General and upon Your Royal Highness as our Masters, by whose blessed arms we are protected, and by whose swords we are defended. Hence, no one need wonder that we shall say daily prayers for Their Excellencies the States General and for Your Highness, and also for the noble governors of this world-renowned city.[5]

In fact, it took more than a decade after the royal visit to Talmud Torah for the Jews in Holland to be accorded the official status of Dutch subjects. This privilege was only granted in 1657, just one year after Oliver Cromwell promised to allow Jews to settle in England, not least because he needed their business to rival that in Amsterdam, and two years after Rabbi Menasseh published his *Humble Addresses to the Lord Protector* in London to promote that cause.

We don't know what the ten-year-old Spinoza made of a Catholic English queen setting foot in the synagogue. But there was another, far more dramatic incident that jolted the Portuguese community and cannot but have left its mark on the boy. It was one of the most shocking events in the short history of the Portuguese synagogue. In 1640, when Spinoza was only eight, a Jew named Uriël da Costa killed himself in a shabby Amsterdam boarding house by firing a bullet through his head. This tragic suicide occurred just a few days after Da Costa had submitted to grotesque humiliations in the synagogue to undo his banishment from the Jewish community. He had to confess to his unspeakable sins for which he deserved to "die a thousand times."[6] These included his violation of the Sabbath, and vile heresies such as his claim that Mosaic law was a human invention. He had even dissuaded two gentiles from converting to the Jewish faith. After confessing, he was forced to strip to the waist, was tied to a pillar, and received thirty-nine lashes with the cantor's leather belt, while a psalm was sung by the devout. Then he had to prostrate himself on the threshold, so that everyone, adults as well as children, could trample on his body.

Even if Spinoza never witnessed this scene, he would certainly have heard about it, since Da Costa had been a notorious figure in Vlooienburg, tormented daily by children of Spinoza's age who threw stones at him and covered him in spit. A Dutch scholar (not Jewish) retold the story with horror in 1896.[7] He ascribed the bigotry behind the cruel ritual of abasement to the influence of the Catholic Inquisition, which had done the Jews such harm. The victims of persecution had become persecutors themselves, Stockholm syndrome avant la lettre, as it were. But the story was more complicated than that. Without considering various angles of the awful Da Costa affair, it is harder to understand what would happen to Spinoza sixteen years later.

Uriël was born in Portugal as Gabriël da Costa to a wealthy, upper-class landowning family. His father was a devout Catholic convert; his mother still clung to remnants of their ancestral Jewish faith. As a young man, Gabriël was instructed in the manners of his class. He rode horses, knew how to wield a sword, and was a pious Catholic, like his father. But he began to have reservations as a law student. His doubts are described in his memoir, published posthumously in 1687, entitled *Example of a Human Life* (Exemplar humanae vitae), the authenticity of which is contested, even though many of his claims are confirmed by others. Da Costa began to regard promises of an afterlife as a fiction. It conflicted with his sense of reason. Searching for more credible routes to the meaning of life, he began, at considerable risk, to delve into Judaism, and came to believe that the Law of Moses was revealed by God. Since adopting the Jewish faith would be much too dangerous in Portugal, Gabriël left his comfortable life behind and moved to Amsterdam, where Jews could at last be Jews again.

He and his four brothers were circumcised in that city, and Gabriël became Uriël. But doubts began to disturb his mind once more. Far from finding the pure faith he was looking for in the synagogue, he was repelled by the endless disputes, rules, and rituals, and the social and intellectual arrogance of the rabbis. He now took up a more radical position: not only Christianity, but Judaism too, was an accumulation of fictions and superstitions that clashed with human reason. He wrote a book, soon to be banned, disputing the immortality of the soul, and he was officially banned from the Jewish community in Hamburg, Venice, and Amsterdam.

Such bans, or *herem*, were not unusual. Many people, even

Rabbi Menasseh, were ostracized for one infringement or another, but usually the *herem* was cast in mild language, and bans rarely lasted long. Rabbi Menasseh was banned for just one day for losing his temper at the council of elders. A person could be put under *herem* for buying kosher meat from an Ashkenazi butcher or for having sexual relations with a gentile—especially serious if this concerned a Jewish woman, less so if it were done by a man. Da Costa's ban was far more serious. He would be "cursed by the law of God." No one, "no matter what their rank," was allowed to speak to him, "whether they be man, woman, parent, or stranger."[8]

When people are banished from their community, or "canceled" as people might now say, they can react in various ways. They can recant, apologize, and ask for forgiveness. They can disappear into obscurity. Or they can double down. Da Costa doubled down. He published a book, explaining once again why the human soul was not immortal and that man-made laws, supposedly handed down from heaven, contradicted the laws of nature. Such views not only outraged the rabbis, but they deeply offended Calvinist beliefs as well. The rabbis denounced Da Costa to the secular authorities in Amsterdam, whereupon he was arrested and thrown in jail. He was released after ten days when two Portuguese sympathizers stood for his bail, and a heavy fine was paid. His critical book, *Examination of the Pharisaic Traditions* (Exame das tradições phariseas) (1623), was burned.

One might argue that rabbinical vindictiveness in seventeenth-century Amsterdam was a kind of mimicry of the Inquisition, but this misses the point of the enforced orthodoxy of that time. Not only did the Jews have to crack down on views expressed by one of their own that would offend the Christians, but they had to be sticklers for rules, laws, and dogmas in a community that had to relearn them, often from scratch. Tolerance was thought to be a luxury they could ill afford. After a history of having to pretend to be better Christians than the Christians, they now had to be perfect Jews. Da Costa was challenging the very foundations of their communal identity, just as Spinoza would do one day. For this, he had to pay a very high price.

Da Costa's search for a faith in God outside the comforting shell of custom or tradition was an early attempt at articulating universal ideas about the human condition, free from tribal loyalties based on culture, religion, or race. But this was not yet possible in the 1620s. Even in a century described by the English philosopher Stuart Hampshire as "the heroic age of modern speculation," a person became socially and spiritually stateless without a religious community. In some sense, one ceased to exist.[9] Da Costa was utterly on his own. Jews scorned him, and Dutch gentiles, whose language he didn't even speak, would have nothing to do with him either. Even his own brothers could not talk to him. He was unable to attend the funeral of his mother at the Jewish cemetery in Ouderkerk. That she, the loving mother of a heretic, was allowed to be buried there at all was a generous concession. His attempt to get married was blocked. No one did business with him. People gathered outside his front door to scream curses at him.

After almost ten years of this, Da Costa couldn't stand it anymore. His isolation had become intolerable, so he looked for a way back into the communal fold. Even if he had to "ape the apes," in his words, it was better to "howl with the wolves" than to be excluded from the pack.[10] His nephew acted as an intermediary. The elders relented. But pretense didn't suit Da Costa's proud nature. The same nephew soon noticed that Da Costa, after the lifting of his ban, wasn't keeping kosher or behaving like a proper Jew. Once again, the fury of the elders came down on him. Mobs were baying for his crucifixion. He was ordered to enter the synagogue, dressed in ashes and sackcloth, or at least in the type of clothes that showed his contrition, and confess his sins with a black candle in his hand. This went too far. He refused to abase himself in this manner.

More years of isolation followed. With barely enough to eat, the ruined man begged to be allowed back in. But he was refused this time, until he finally agreed in 1640 to undergo the humiliating rituals of atonement that involved the public flogging and trampling over his body on the threshold of the synagogue. Clearly, the shame of this degrading episode was too much for Da Costa, who could no longer bear to be alive.

No doubt, most people would have seen Da Costa's behavior as reckless, needlessly stubborn, perhaps even arrogant. Why couldn't he just conform and keep his thoughts to himself? Judaism can be relatively relaxed about religious doubters, so long as they observe the rules. Surely, Da Costa's first duty to himself was to survive. But there was something heroic about his refusal to bow to the demands of men whose dogmas he found absurd.

We don't know for sure what lessons Spinoza might have drawn from Uriël da Costa's tragic fate. But the ring that Spinoza wore and used to seal his letters gives us a clue. It shows his initials, BDS, and the image of a rose with thorns—*Espinoza* or *Espinho* means "thorn" in Portuguese. And underneath the thorny flower is the Latin word *Caute*—meaning "beware," or "be cautious." Spinoza would be more cautious than Da Costa had been. But if Da Costa was heroic in his insistence to think for himself, Spinoza's courage was even more remarkable, as we will see.

4

———◆◆◆◆———

Driven Out of the Temple

Quite when Spinoza started having his own religious doubts is hard to know. They must have crept up on him. There was no Eureka moment. Jean Maximilien Lucas, a French Protestant refugee who had known Spinoza well, wrote an admiring—even somewhat gushing—account of the philosopher's life soon after his death. He assumed that the young Spinoza had been much too brilliant to be satisfied with the Hebrew teachings of his schooldays. Barely fifteen years old, Spinoza supposedly raised questions that "even the most learned Jews had trouble answering." Indeed, Lucas thought, his precocious doubts must have embarrassed his teachers. Still, said Lucas, Spinoza's teacher, Rabbi Morteira, could not help but respect "the comportment and genius" of his young pupil.[1] Well, perhaps so.

Little about this time of Spinoza's life is certain, but it is possible that he attended Keter Torah, the yeshiva run by Rabbi Morteira, after leaving the Talmud Torah school in the early

1650s. His formal schooling ended presumably because his father needed his help to run the family business. Indeed, the business was not going very well. The long war with Spain had finally ended in the Peace of Münster in 1648. But war with England four years later meant that Dutch cargo ships carrying goods from Portugal or North Africa were often raided at sea. The English parliament banned the Dutch from trading in the English Caribbean colonies, cutting off another lucrative source of income. Pirates from the Barbary coast looted ships full of cargo. And Michael's company was still laden with debts, some taken on for the sake of others, some owed to crypto-Jewish businessmen in France.

Spinoza's younger brother, Gabriel, might have been suited to business. Spinoza was not. But various disasters in the family meant that he had to try. First, Spinoza's sister Miriam died. The next to go, in 1653, was Michael's third wife, Spinoza's stepmother, Esther, who had already been ill for some time. All this, as well as business failures, must have been exhausting. In the following year, Michael himself was dead. The family firm now continued as "Bento y Gabriel d'Espinoza."

How much money was passed on to Michael's children, and how it was distributed, is yet another hazy episode in Spinoza's life. One story is probably apocryphal, but it is worth retelling, as it suggests that Spinoza had a practical side, that he was more than a bookish thinker with his head in the clouds. The story goes that his sister (or possibly half-sister) Rebecca and her husband, a rabbinical student named Samuel de Casseres, conspired to take for themselves what was Spinoza's due. Spinoza decided he wouldn't stand for this and took them to court. Once the court found that he had the right to his inheritance, Spinoza, having made his point, left everything to his sister and her husband—everything except his parents' bed, the one in which his mother had died, and which he carried with him whenever he moved to another house. The part about the bed might be true. If not, the story, as the Italians say, is "well contrived." According to all accounts it must indeed have been a fine bed, apparently with dark-green velvet curtains.[2]

Other accounts, perhaps more reliable, say that Spinoza had inherited money from his mother, but nothing from his father, apart from some serious debts. Since his mother's money was tied up in his father's estate, Spinoza initially agreed to pay what his father owed. When this proved to be an uphill task, he tried something else. As he was not yet twenty-five, and thus legally a minor, he could be declared an orphan and be released from the obligation to take care of his father's debts. This matter was apparently concluded to his satisfaction, which has led to speculation that these shadowy financial deals were the reason for Spinoza's excommunication from the Jewish community— that, and his steadily dwindling cash contributions to the Portuguese Nation. Given the ferocity of the ban, and the fact that there was probably nothing illegal about Spinoza's affairs, this explanation seems implausible. But he might well have offended the nation by using a Dutch civilian court and not the Jewish authorities to extricate himself from his father's liabilities. He had done nothing to break the Dutch laws; Jewish laws were another matter.

That Spinoza preferred a life of quiet contemplation to the rough and tumble of commerce must have been obvious early on. Lucas wrote that "men who had done business with [Michael], realizing that his son was not one to let them get away with their swindles, made life so difficult for [Spinoza] that he preferred to let them keep everything rather than sacrifice his peace of mind for the sake of false hope."[3]

The documented case of the Alvares brothers appears to confirm this assessment of Spinoza's character. Anthony and Gabriel Alvares, men of low reputation, owed the Spinozas money for a jewelry transaction. But the debt was never paid; there was always another excuse for putting it off. Spinoza went to court.

Anthony was arrested and confined to an inn called the Four Hollanders, in the center of Amsterdam. As soon as Spinoza entered the inn to collect his debt, Anthony knocked him on the head with his fist. On his way out, Gabriel lay in wait for him and hit him so hard that Spinoza's hat fell into the gutter. Despite this rough treatment, Spinoza was obliged to pay the costs of Anthony's arrest. After some more negotiation, the Alvares brothers agreed to take care of these fees. But Spinoza, again perhaps to be freed from further aggravation, lent them more money to do so. There is no record of the original debt ever being repaid.

Spinoza wrote about worldly ambitions in the *Treatise on the Emendation of the Intellect* (Tractatus de intellectus emendatione), published posthumously. Looking back, he gives hints of his state of mind as a businessman. He wrote: "The mind is distracted not a little by the pursuit of honors and wealth, particularly when the latter is sought only for its own sake, because it is assumed to be the highest good." Furthermore, Spinoza said that "honor has this great disadvantage: to pursue it, we must direct our lives according to other men's powers of understanding— fleeing what they commonly flee and seeking what they commonly seek."[4]

Spinoza sent a letter to a Mennonite friend in 1671, in which he fiercely criticized a pamphlet entitled *Political Man* (Homo politicus) (unknown).[5] This pernicious work, he said, was written to instruct people how to achieve money and status. How much wiser, he continued, was the ancient Greek sage, Thales of Miletus, who said that wise men didn't lack in wealth because of failure, but out of choice. When one of his friends sneered at his poverty, Thales set out to prove that he could be rich if he wanted to be. As a seasoned astrologer, he could tell that, unlike in previous years of scarcity, the following year would bring an abundance of olives. So, he rented all the olive presses in Greece cheaply and then made a killing by renting them out to others for a much higher price. Once he was a rich man, he gave all his money away. Spinoza's own failure as a merchant could not be pressed so easily into a high-minded story like that, but he might have fancied himself as a sage in the tradition of Thales. At the very least, he resented being thought of as a soft touch.

Engaging in the family business didn't mean that Spinoza stopped studying, at Morteira's yeshiva or possibly with another teacher. He still conformed to the practices of his faith, saying kaddish for his father in the synagogue, and so on. But a growing sense of alienation came from his independence of mind and exposure to wider ideas through his extensive reading and his growing acquaintance with people outside his narrow Sephardic community, some of whom he met while doing business at the Amsterdam stock exchange. Exactly what his major influences were, and whom he met, when, and where, are matters of contention. When did he first engage with the ideas of René Descartes? We don't know for sure. How influential was his Latin teacher, Franciscus van den Enden? Did he even know him before the ban in 1656? Probably. Were some of the sources of his rebellion against Judaism to be found in Jewish philosophy itself? All this may be speculated upon. And speculate many people have to this day: the great Spinoza scholar Jonathan Israel thinks that Spinoza's early rebellion came largely off his own bat.[6] Spinoza's biographer Steven Nadler believes that Van den Enden's schooling was "of crucial importance to his intellectual and personal development."[7]

We know that Spinoza was interested in science. Studying medicine was common among Jews. Many of Spinoza's friends were medical doctors of one kind or another. We also know that Descartes, who wrote his major works in the Dutch Republic in the 1630s and 1640s, was known to all educated Dutch citizens, some of whom revered him, and some of whom thought he was sent to Holland by the devil. Educated by Jesuits, Descartes came to live and work among the Dutch, because there he could think and write more freely than in France. As Nadler puts it nicely: "If one must search for the 'corrupter' of Spinoza, then, in a sense the real culprit is Amsterdam itself."[8] Amsterdam was not just Mokum, the city of refuge, for Jews, but also for Huguenots, Quakers, and other victims of persecution; it was known in the seventeenth century as Vrijstad, meaning "Freetown," or, in Greek, Eleutheropolis—a city of publishers, art dealers, printers, painters' studios, and bookshops where free spirits gathered to discuss ideas that could land a person in prison or on the stake in other parts of Europe. Such gatherings were condemned by the Calvinist clergy, but the city's patrician regents usually turned a blind eye to them—again, *gedoogd*, or tolerated, would be the right word to describe this. Some city fathers were even quite sympathetic to new ideas.

The last year of Michael Spinoza's life, 1653, was also when the most distinguished Dutch patrician, Johan ("Jan") de Witt, became grand pensionary, the highest official in the Dutch Republic, ushering in two decades of relatively liberal rule. His brother, Cornelis, was effectively his minister of the interior, in charge of the police. William II of Orange had launched a military coup against the States General in 1650, which ended in an embarrassing failure when his troops did not succeed in their march on Amsterdam. He died later that same year. Because his dynastic successor, his son William, was still a baby, the regents grabbed their chance to do without a stadtholder altogether. Joost van den Vondel, the most famous playwright of the Dutch Golden Age, whom Johan de Witt appointed as the republic's first poet laureate, compared the fate of William II, and the Orange dynasty with him, to that of Phaeton, who crashed to earth in the flaming chariot of his father, Helios, the sun god. De Witt would own some of Spinoza's books, even though he didn't agree with everything they contained. He was also a decent mathematician.

The most famous publisher, printer, and bookseller of radical, "dangerous" books, including works by Descartes and later Spinoza himself, was Jan Rieuwertsz, a native of Amsterdam. His shop, called the Book of Martyrs, was where freethinkers met to discuss science, politics, and religion, much to the horror of Calvinist authorities, who kept complaining to the city authorities about such devilish goings-on. Some of these free spirits were Remonstrants, some would have called themselves libertines, some were Quakers, who arrived from England, but most were Mennonites, like Rieuwertsz himself. These young Mennonites who defied their older, more conservative brethren were not atheists, but relatively broad-minded Christian humanists. The leading figure among these liberal Mennonites was a young minister named Galenus Abrahamsz de Haan, who organized meetings with kindred spirits at his family home, and sometimes in Mennonite church halls, which greatly upset his more conservative brethren.

Galenus, who began his career as a medical doctor, rejected the official Christian denominations, including his own church, as the true temples of God. Christianity, he believed, had been corrupted by too much ritual and clerical obscurantism. Everyone should be free to follow the example of Christ's life; faith was something to be personally experienced and not imposed as an official dogma. A friendly theologian in his circle named Adam Boreel saw the Bible as the only source of authority; religion should be practiced freely and in private. Old school Mennonites denounced Galenus and his friends as "Socinianists." Like the Mennonites, Socinianists refused to swear oaths or bear arms, and they rejected the Holy Trinity and the notion of predestination. Galenus was certainly close to the Socinianists. He was also part of the Collegiants, an informal association (or college, hence the name) of Arminians and other Protestant dissenters, who would meet in various private places on Sunday afternoons to discuss matters freely, without bothering about orthodoxy of any kind. Vondel, the playwright, came from a

Mennonite family, even though he later, rather eccentrically, converted to Catholicism. Some Mennonite businessmen, including several of Spinoza's friends, were rich, but it mustn't be forgotten that like Catholics and Jews, Mennonites were only *gedoogd* without having all the rights of orthodox Christians; they were still barred from government jobs.

Other Mennonites who came to smoke and drink and argue at the Book of Martyrs included Isaac and Simon Joosten de Vries, both wealthy Amsterdam merchants related to Vondel. Then there was Pieter Balling, who spoke Spanish, and Jarig Jellesz, a bachelor who gave up his grocery business to dedicate his life to philosophical reflection. As a good, sober Mennonite, Jellesz dressed simply in black cloth. So did Spinoza, but his style still bore the traces of his Spanish heritage; his dark clothes were more finely cut from better material and his shoes had silver buckles. This, then, was the milieu in which the young Spinoza began to feel comfortable. Some of its members became lifelong friends. He had already met Balling, Jellesz, and the De Vries brothers at the bourse. It was most probably they who drew him into the Book of Martyrs circle. Spinoza might have spoken to Balling in Spanish, but he would have conversed with his other friends in Dutch.

Lucas relates about this period that Spinoza had had "so little intercourse with the Jews for some time that he was obliged to associate with Christians, and he formed ties of friendship with intellectual people who told him that it was a pity that he knew neither Greek nor Latin."[9] Those intellectuals, for their part, would have been interested in Spinoza's knowledge of Hebrew, which helped them to interpret the Old Testament with greater expertise.

There are different accounts about who first taught Spinoza Latin. Johannes Colerus, a German Lutheran minister who moved to The Hague just after Spinoza died, believed that a German student was Spinoza's first teacher. But he is the only one to say so. A more likely teacher was Franciscus van den Enden, a Flemish ex-Jesuit, who was apparently thrown out of the order for displaying too much fondness for the wife of an army officer; he was later denounced for preaching free love. There is no agreement among Spinoza scholars about the beginning of Van den Enden's Latin lessons to Spinoza. Some claim they only started after Spinoza's *herem*.[10] But most think instruction must have begun earlier. This seems likely.

Van den Enden was in any case a remarkable figure. Born in 1602 in Antwerp, he died rather unfortunately in 1674, when he was hanged in front of the Bastille for plotting against Louis XIV. Educated first by the Franciscans and later by the Jesuits, Van den Enden studied to be a physician. He may have practiced as a doctor, but his main business in Antwerp was publishing and selling fine art, chiefly prints by Rubens and other Flemish masters. He married in 1641 and had a daughter named Clara Maria, after her mother. Around 1645 the family moved to Amsterdam, supposedly because Van den Enden's liberal ideas had made him dangerous enemies in Antwerp, a city still firmly under Spanish rule. A more prosaic explanation is that moving to the Dutch Republic offered better business opportunities. His print and book shop in Amsterdam, named In the Art Shop (In den Konstwinkel), was one of the fixtures of "Freetown," where people would meet socially, as well as browse in risky books. Van den Enden knew many of Spinoza's friends. They frequented the same places. Perhaps he was more interested in ideas than in running a business, for his shop soon went bust. But he was saved from financial ruin by rich friends. To make ends meet, Van den Enden then opened a Latin school, which was popular with children from well-to-do families who found the traditional Latin schools too stuffy. His daughter Clara Maria was such a brilliant Latinist at the age of twelve that she was his teaching assistant. She also gave singing lessons and was apparently blessed with such charm that people forgot that she was lame. She may well have taught Spinoza too. Nothing is known about the quality of his singing, or if he sang very much at all.

Spinoza owned Latin dictionaries printed before the 1650s, and he may well have started learning Latin quite early on. He knew that this was essential for gaining access to scientific and philosophical ideas (there was in fact no clear distinction between the two in the seventeenth century). His Jewish teachers knew this too. Rabbis Morteira and Menasseh both read Latin. Neither was unaware of modern ideas either. Menasseh was even quite friendly with Adam Boreel, the "Socinianist" Mennonite. What Van den Enden taught Spinoza apart from Latin at this stage is less clear. He was later accused of poisoning the minds of his pupils with atheism, but since he at least observed the forms of his Catholic faith, and had sold many prints with religious themes, this may just have been malicious gossip. His living room was decorated with a picture of Jesus. He might have introduced Spinoza early on to the works of Descartes, Bacon, Hobbes, and, especially Machiavelli, who was one of his favorite authors. But even without his introduction, Spinoza would have been familiar with some of these thinkers. After all, the Dutch air was thick with Descartes's ideas. However, Van den Enden's radical notions about political freedom and democracy, which resembled Spinoza's politics, only came later, well after Spinoza's *herem*. By then, it was hard to tell which of the two had exerted the greater influence on the other.

Van den Enden in the 1650s was above all a humanist, deeply in love with classical texts and the Italian Renaissance. He was also a man of the theater, and he delighted in putting on plays in Latin and Greek. A favorite piece was *Andria*, by Terence, who coined the famous dictum that nothing human was alien to him. Terence's comedy about various amorous misunderstandings was revived and adapted as a popular play by Machiavelli. When Van den Enden planned to perform *Andria* with his students at Amsterdam's Municipal Theater in 1656, the year of Spinoza's ban, the Calvinists were up in arms, partly because they disapproved of any type of theater (apart from preaching and singing in church), but mostly because Van den Enden decided to have the female roles acted not by boys, as was customary, but by actual women. As usual, the city authorities chose to look the other way—and not always even that, as some came to the opening night.

Spinoza's love of the theater and classical literature was certainly encouraged by Van den Enden. He performed in some of the plays himself and would quote or paraphrase his favorite Latin authors extensively in his later works. Like his teacher, Spinoza was fond of the Stoics, such as Cicero and Seneca. Allusions to Terence also pop up in odd places. In a letter to his friend Lodewijk Meijer (yet another physician/philosopher) in 1663, Spinoza launches into a philosophical disquisition on the impossibility to imagine "substance" (that is, God's imminence in nature) and infinity.[11] What Spinoza did in this letter is quite remarkable. He appears to have taken a passage from Terence's comedy *The Eunuch* (Eunuchus), in which a shrewd slave gives some sound advice to an Athenian youth in love with a foreign courtesan, and then rephrased it as a metaphysical problem. Here are the words of the slave: "In love there are all these evils; wrongs, suspicions, enmities, reconcilements, war, then peace; if you expect to render these things, naturally uncertain, certain by dint of reason, you wouldn't effect it a bit the more than if you were to use your endeavors to be mad with reason."[12] And here is Spinoza: "For since there are many things which we cannot at all grasp by the imagination, but only by the intellect (such as Substance, Eternity, etc.), if someone strives to explain such things by Notions of this kind, which are only aids to the Imagination, he will accomplish nothing more than if he takes pains to go mad with his imagination."[13]

The amorous heart of a young Athenian is far from Spinoza's concept of God or nature, or indeed infinity, but he makes the point, often repeated in his later writings, that there are different ways to acquire knowledge. One is through the imagination, another is by human reason, and a third way to grasp reality is by intuition. But these methods to gain knowledge should be applied always in their proper places. You can't rationalize love, and you can't imagine infinity.

His teacher's introduction to the classics of Rome and Greece was not the only possible spur to Spinoza's critical faculties. Other heretical ideas, apart from Descartes, were swirling around the bookshops of Amsterdam at the time. A French Protestant named Isaac de la Peyrère, for example, shocked and excited many Europeans when he published his book *The Pre-Adamites* (Prae-Adamitae) anonymously in Holland in 1655. Like many freethinkers, he enjoyed the financial support of Queen Christina of Sweden, "the Minerva of the North," who cultivated an intellectually libertine atmosphere at her court. In fact, the book had been circulating in manuscript form already for some time. Peyrère, a diplomat and "erudite libertine," probably with Marrano family roots, argued that the Pentateuch could not have been written by Moses; that Adam, far from being the first person to be alive, was born long after American tribes and other non-Jewish people had been around; and that Israel was not nearly as old as China.

This inflammatory treatise was burned in Rome, and Peyrère was locked up in prison for six months "as a Jew and a Protestant" by the archbishop of the Southern Netherlands, then under Spanish rule. While in prison, he was forced to convert to the Catholic faith. But before this unlucky turn of events, he had visited Amsterdam, where he interested Rabbi Menasseh in another of his ideas, which was that a Jewish messiah would soon liberate the Holy Land with the help of the prince of Condé, the Protestant pretender to the French throne, and form a world government. This last notion may not have held any special appeal to Spinoza. But Spinoza did own a copy of *The*

Pre-Adamites, which shows that his biblical criticism didn't appear in a vacuum.

In fact, Spinoza's criticism was not only inspired by reading Latin authors and consorting with Christian dissenters. Already before that, he was reading Jewish philosophers who had broken the bounds of orthodoxy. Steven Nadler mentions two seminal works: Maimonides's *Guide of the Perplexed* (Dalālat al-ḥā'irīn) (1190), and Judah Abrabanel's *Dialogues on Love* (Dialoghi d'amore) (1535). Both authors, one in the twelfth century and the other in the sixteenth, tried to solve the tensions between faith and reason by finding rational explanations for obscure or contradictory passages in the scripture. Spinoza thought this was a futile enterprise. But his thinking does show influences of another kind. Maimonides argued strenuously against the conception of God as a corporal or moral being. God is neither good or bad, joyful or angry, wise or unwise. He is not like a human being in any sense. But there can be an understanding of God through our intelligence. Since not all men are intelligent enough to gain such understanding, Maimonides believed that philosophy could dangerously confuse untutored minds and should be left to the learned. Unlike Maimonides, Spinoza's idea of the learned was not defined by knowledge of and belief in the sacred Jewish texts, but his fear of exposing the masses to philosophy was similar. Abrabanel's influence was perhaps not so stringent. He might have struck a different chord in Spinoza by enriching the Jewish tradition with a strong dose of Italian Renaissance humanism.

Before his ban, Spinoza also consorted with Jews who shared some of his doubts. One fellow pupil at Rabbi Morteira's Keter Torah yeshiva was a particularly tragic case. He was a Spanish Marrano named Juan de Prado, who had studied medicine at the University of Toledo. But life in Spain under the Inquisition became too dangerous after one of his relatives confessed under torture that Prado had been proselytizing fellow Marranos, trying to persuade them to live as Jews. He moved to Rome as the personal physician to the archbishop of Seville, and from Rome to Hamburg, where he joined the Sephardic community, and Juan became Daniel. In 1655 he settled as a doctor in Amsterdam and studied at the yeshiva.

Despite his desire to live as a Jew, secretly in Spain, openly in Hamburg and Amsterdam, Dr. Prado had doubts about the rules, regulations, and dogmas of the religion he had so hopefully embraced. He found what he was taught at the yeshiva narrow-minded and constricting. Why should the Jewish people have a monopoly on God? Why was it necessary to stick to all those dietary restrictions? Wasn't it possible to break away from Jewish orthodoxy and still live as a Jew? The answer in the seventeenth century, especially in a community of defensive Sephardic immigrants, was that it was not. If you wished to remain part of the community, you had to abide by its rules. If you chose not to, you were on your own.

Prado and Spinoza would have been kindred spirits in 1655, and their doubts were most probably aired in Rabbi Morteira's classes. Indeed, one suspects that both men were a pain in the rabbi's neck. That they attended his class is strongly suggested by an account of the yeshiva written by a poet named Daniel Levi de Barrios. De Barrios was an odd figure. Born in Spain to Marranos, he formally took up the Jewish faith in Italy after fleeing the Inquisition. He would have serious bouts of insanity, when he refused to eat, was an ardent follower of the false messiah Sabbatai Tzvi, and wrote about the yeshiva in Amsterdam six years after Spinoza's death. He also made his living writing poems in praise of European monarchs. Still, there is no reason to think that he made the following up:

> The Crown of the Law [Keter Torah], ever since the year of
> its joyous foundation, never ceased burning in the academic
> bush, thanks to the doctrinal leaves written by the most wise

Saul Levi Morteira, lending his intellect to the counsel of Wisdom and his pen to the hand of Speculation, in the defense of religion and against atheism. *Thorns* are they that, in the *Fields* of impiety, aim to shine with the fire that consumes them.[14]

The English word *thorn* is *Espina* in Spanish, and *prado* means "field." Spinoza and Prado were embarrassing their teacher. Rabbi Morteira was so worried about his clever but difficult student that he decided to draw him out by rather devious means (or so Lucas would have us believe; it may be true). Two young men were sent to Spinoza to trick him into revealing what he really thought about the Jewish faith. Looking shifty, they asked him leading questions about his views on God's corporality, the existence of angels, or the immortality of the soul. Spinoza, clearly aware of the risks of speaking too freely about such matters to strangers, gave them evasive answers. According to Lucas, his most sympathetic biographer, Spinoza's "love of the truth was such that he avoided contact with almost everyone."[15] Spinoza said that since there was nothing in the scripture to suggest that God had no body, one might well believe that he did. As far as the soul was concerned, he said that since the word referred to life and everything that was alive, there was no need to find proof for its immortality.

These answers failed to satisfy Spinoza's interlocutors. Why they then began to spread rumors among the Sephardim that Spinoza was a godless man, who made a mockery of his faith, is not explained. But when these rumors reached the ears of the council of elders, the *ma'amad*, they were so concerned that they summoned Spinoza to give an account of himself. They warned him of the consequences if the rumors were true; he could be banned from the synagogue as a heretic. Spinoza assured the elders of his innocence. Whereupon the two young witnesses who had been sent to question him shouted (still according to Lucas)

that Spinoza had mocked the Jews as an ignorant and superstitious people who knew nothing about God, but still claimed
him as their own. Not just that, but Spinoza had had the audac-
ity to claim that the laws of Moses were made by men, that angels were figments of the imagination, and that the immortality
of the soul was a lie. "Anathema!" cried the elders. What did the
accused have to say for himself? Spinoza answered that all this
fuss made him feel sorry for them, and that he would be happy
to say amen to the stories of such fine witnesses.

Whether Spinoza really said these things can't be proven,
but the accusations ring true, since they merely stated what Spinoza professed to believe ever since, and most probably believed
then. Spinoza made things worse for himself when, according
to Lucas, Rabbi Morteira joined the meeting and asked him to
choose between offering a sincere apology and repent his er-
rant ways or be banned from the community.

Now, Spinoza often advocated prudence during his life. He
refused to attach his name to his radical publications for fear of
retribution, and he refused to have them translated from Latin
into more accessible Dutch. Whether or not dissembling was
part of his Marrano heritage, he tried to avoid needlessly provoking the fury of zealots. But he would not apologize for what
he believed. In fact, if Lucas is to be trusted, he couldn't help
himself and provoked his rabbi even more, by saying that he
was perfectly aware of the seriousness of the threatened ban,
and "would be happy to repay Rabbi Morteira's many lessons in
Hebrew by instructing him on the correct form of the *herem*."[16]

Johannes Colerus, the Lutheran pastor, claimed that despite this insult, Rabbi Morteira did everything to keep Spinoza within the Jewish fold. Spinoza himself is said to have told
his last landlord in The Hague that he was offered a generous
yearly stipend of one thousand guilders if only he would conform to the customs and laws of his ancestors. If he would keep
his doubts to himself, the elders could live with that. Perhaps

he was offered such a deal because of his intellectual brilliance. It is more likely, however, that everything was done to avoid a scandal that could cause a great deal of trouble and draw unwelcome attention from the gentiles. It was bad enough that some Jews were converting to Christianity—with the encouragement of Calvinists. In any case, Spinoza refused to submit to such hypocrisy, not even, as he supposedly told his landlord, for ten thousand guilders.

Leaving a strict religious community is never easy. There is always a high price to pay, which can entail serious violence. Pierre Bayle, the French Huguenot thinker who fled to Holland in the 1680s, wrote in his famous *Historical and Critical Dictionary* (Dictionnaire historique et critique) of 1697 that Spinoza was knifed by a furious young Jewish zealot shortly after his interrogation in the synagogue. This supposedly happened as Spinoza emerged from the theater. Colerus reports that the attack occurred at the gate of the Portuguese synagogue. Whichever the location, the wound was slight, and perhaps the knife even missed its mark. But, assuming the story to be true, the assault contributed to Spinoza's final rupture with his Jewish community, which Bayle believes led to his formal banishment. Bayle tried to figure out the exact circumstances, without success. Spinoza's own apologia in Spanish was apparently lost, but, in Bayle's words, "all the seeds of atheism were slipped into [Spinoza's] *Theological-Political Treatise*, a pernicious and detestable book published in Amsterdam in 1670."[17]

5

The Dark Years

THE YEAR 1656 was the best of times in some ways and the worst of times in others. The Republic of the United Netherlands was firmly in the hands of the grand pensionary, Johan de Witt, and the regents. The republic had fought a nasty little war with England in 1652 and 1653, largely over commercial interests, and lost. When peace was negotiated, Oliver Cromwell insisted that the House of Orange be excluded from public office. The Orangists, after all, had been on the royalist side in the English Civil War. And the last stadtholder of the Netherlands, William II, was the son-in-law of Charles I. Cromwell even suggested a union between the two Protestant trading nations, as a bulwark against the monarchies of Europe.

De Witt had no interest in an Anglo-Dutch union, but he was receptive to the idea of taking out the House of Orange. He could use Cromwell's demand to his advantage in the continuing rivalry between the urban regent class, mostly in Holland, and the Orangists and their Calvinist supporters in other provinces. (In some ways, the Dutch Republic was more like the European Union, with its many overlapping and sometimes conflicting sources of political authority, than a modern nation-state.) The Act of Seclusion in 1654 abolished the stadtholder. The Orange-colored provinces were too weak to protest.

Unlike Cromwell, De Witt was never a dictator, let alone a military strongman. He believed in divided powers, shared responsibilities, and at least the appearance of consensus. Each sovereign province of the republic had its own government; conflicts of interest would be thrashed out in meetings of the States-General (a bit like the European Council in the EU), meetings that went on and on, and on. Rule by regents was not a system that rewarded high office to men of wealth or aristocratic bloodlines. Virtue and propriety were the marks of political legitimacy. A stadtholder or a king might lead a dissolute life in brothels and gambling halls, but not an upright Protestant regent. Projecting himself as the most virtuous, most far-seeing, most competent regent, De Witt's authority was for a while unassailable. He, and his brother Cornelis, who was his closest adviser, represented what they called True Freedom, rule by a virtuous patriciate. The Dutch Golden Age was no democracy, but it allowed philosophers to develop their ideas in relative freedom, a freedom that Spinoza did everything in his writings to promote and protect.

Like other parts of Europe, however, the Dutch Republic was ravaged by the plague in 1655 and 1656. Dead bodies with buboes as big as apples were piled up high outside the many churches that dotted the skyline of Dutch towns. People fought over coffins, which had become scarce. Medical doctors believed that the black death came from toxic air. The stench of rotting bodies was so bad that vats of saltpeter and brimstone were burned in the hope of clearing the atmosphere. Tobacco was also assumed to have a detoxifying effect. Calvinist preachers thundered from the pulpits that the plague was God's punishment for man's sinfulness. It was all the whoring and drinking in big cities that had brought on the Lord's wrath. Rich people, including Sephardic families, fled from their townhouses along the fetid canals of Amsterdam to their country villas along the Amstel River or the Vecht—where many of these fine houses still stand. Roughly 10 percent of the population in cities such as Leiden and Amsterdam died of the plague. Church bells tolled incessantly. The daily death toll was chalked up on a board outside the town hall. All people could do was to wrap their faces in scarves. Panic or any sign of fear was considered by doctors to make people more vulnerable to the deadly disease.

Spinoza's *herem* took place in front of the Ark of the Torah at the Portuguese synagogue on July 27, 1656, when the summer heat must have made plague-ridden Amsterdam almost insufferable. Jean Maximilien Lucas describes perhaps with a little too much relish the rituals that took place when a blasphemer was banned from the Portuguese synagogue: the *hazzan* would intone the words of the *herem* in a gloomy voice, while the wax from black candles was dripped into a bowl of blood. And the devout, ignited by a holy rage, would doubtless tear the blasphemer apart, if he fell into their hands.

But Spinoza was not present during his ban, which was probably just as well. The *herem* might have been read aloud in Portuguese by Rabbi Aboab. It isn't clear whether Rabbi Morteira was there. Rabbi Menasseh was absent from the proceedings, since he was busy dining with Cromwell in London. There were no black candles or bowls of blood. But the words of the *herem* were chilling:

> With the judgment of the angels and with that of the saints, we put under *herem*, ostracize and curse and damn Baruch de Espinoza, with the consent of the Blessed God and with the consent of this entire holy congregation, before these holy scrolls, with the 613 precepts which are written in them; with

the *herem* that Joshua put upon Jericho, with the curse with which Elisha cursed the youth, and with all the curses that are written in the law. Cursed be he by day and cursed be he by night; cursed be he when he lies down and cursed be he when he rises up. Cursed be he when he goes out and cursed be he when he comes in. The Lord will not forgive him. The fury and zeal of the Lord will burn against this man and bring upon him all the curses that are written in this book of the law. And may the Lord separate him for evil from all the tribes of Israel, with all the curses of the covenant that are written in this book of the law. And you that cleave unto the Lord your God, all of you are alive today.[1]

This was a fiercer ban than the one imposed on Spinoza's friend Dr. Juan de Prado, even after the latter was excommunicated for the second time in 1658. Unlike Spinoza, Dr. Prado was accused of openly mocking Jewish laws and writing "scandalous and immoral" letters to be deposited in Morteira's yeshiva. Consequently, the board of directors, the *ma'amad*, decided, "with the advice of the rabbis," that Prado be "separated from the Nation," and that all Jews, apart from members of his family, would be forbidden to contact him.[2]

This was much softer than all the curses thrown at Spinoza, who was not allowed even to meet his own siblings. His brother Gabriel now had to carry on the family firm on his own. Most Jews who were banned were expected to return to the fold after they had shown sufficient remorse. Spinoza was booted out of his community without any expectation of him ever coming back. One of the great questions hanging over Spinoza's life is why the words of his *herem* were so harsh. We know where the text came from. To settle an earlier dispute in the Amsterdam Portuguese community, concerning rabbinical authority, Rabbi Morteira had traveled to Venice in 1618 to seek advice from the Venetian rabbis. They came up with the words for a *herem* that were later used in Spinoza's case. Drawn from a thirteenth-century text on Jewish customs, this *herem* was meant for people who "sowed the seeds of schism."[3]

Spinoza could not really be accused of sowing the seeds of schism. Despite his dwindling financial contributions to the nation, possibly due to a downturn in his business, he had been dutiful in his religious observances. He hadn't, so far as we know, bought meat from Ashkenazic, let alone nonkosher butchers. He hadn't attempted to convert anyone to Christianity. He hadn't worshipped idols or sacrificed to other gods. He certainly hadn't been known for any lewd behavior, in public or in private. He had perhaps discussed theological matters with the gentiles, which was forbidden, but so had Rabbi Menasseh, and arguably even Rabbi Morteira, in his dismissal of Beelthouwer's arguments in the synagogue. The elders spoke of Spinoza's "evil opinions and acts," of his "abominable heresies" and "monstrous deeds," but they did not explain what these actions and opinions were.[4] So why the venom? Many explanations have been advanced.

One of the least persuasive claims is that the Jews in Amsterdam were particularly sensitive to Spinoza's alleged heresies just as Rabbi Menasseh was negotiating with Cromwell about a Jewish return to England. Another explanation concerns commercial interests. War with England had been the cause of bankruptcies. Rabbi Aboab and senior members of the *ma'amad* were influential businessmen with shares in the Dutch West India Company. They might have been concerned to keep tight control over Jewish business interests by insisting on solidarity among members of the Portuguese Nation. Spinoza's many dealings with gentiles might have been seen as a challenge to the *ma'amad*.

Then there is the question of legal authority. By going to a Dutch civil court to sort out problems with his father's inheritance, Spinoza had undermined the authority of the men presiding over the Jewish community, which was governed by different laws.[5] But even if this had been an issue, it alone is unlikely to account for the extreme wording of his *herem*.

A clue might lie in the case that prompted Rabbi Morteira to seek the counsel of the Venetian rabbis in 1618. The Sephardim in Amsterdam had been split into two camps, one following a physician named David Farrar, and the other supporting a rabbi named Joseph Pardo. Farrar had opposed the appointment of Pardo. The assignment of clerics often sparked rows in the seventeenth-century Netherlands, among Jews as much as among the Protestants. In the Jewish community, this involved the right to ban people for bad behavior or heresies as well. Did the rabbis or the lay officials have this right?[6] Bringing Pardo as a rabbi to Amsterdam was particularly fraught because he had been arrested in Venice for not paying his debts. But bad debts cannot have been the only reason for Farrar's resistance.

Farrar, a Marrano born and bred as a Christian in Portugal, only became a pious Jew in Amsterdam, insisting on wearing fringed garments every day and never drinking impure wine. He was, in a sense, more Jewish than "many of those circumcised from birth" (in the words of Leon of Modena, the famous Venetian rabbi).[7] He also had a reputation as an intellectual and a bit of a maverick. A bit like many Protestant dissidents, Farrar resented the power of rabbis; the road to God had to be a private affair; religion was to be practiced and not imposed by religious authorities, corrupted by superstitions and frippery to bamboozle simpler minds into subservience.

As an independent thinker, as well as a religious purist, Farrar didn't want rabbis to interfere with his own interpretations of the Jewish faith. This was like Dr. Juan de Prado's later descriptions of the Amsterdam rabbinate as a kind of Inquisition. Such men did not want the rabbis to act as censors of free thought. One might call them Jewish Protestants.

Spinoza was never devout, like Farrar, or deliberately provocative, like Dr. Prado, but the rabbis still saw his intellectual independence as a threat. That he was neither religious, in any conventional sense, nor interested in living as a Jew, might have made him an even greater menace in rabbinical eyes than Prado or Farrar, for he had slipped out of their control. This might explain why Farrar was never expelled and Prado's ban was less severe. Rabbi Morteira had even praised Farrar's critical spirit. Farrar, after all, was still a pious Jew. Whereas Prado kept begging the board of the synagogue to let him back in, and was prepared to mouth the required apologies, Spinoza's attitude couldn't have been more different. After being informed of his *herem*, he said, according to Lucas:

> They do not force me to do anything that I would not have done of my own accord if I did not dread scandal; but since they want it that way, I enter gladly on the path that is opened to me, with the consolation that my departure will be more innocent than was the exodus of the early Hebrews from Egypt. Although my subsistence is no better secured than was theirs, I take away nothing from anybody and, whatever injustice may be done to me, I can boast that people have nothing to reproach me with.[8]

This still leaves the question why the *ma'amad* and the rabbis were so intensely disturbed by Spinoza's heresies. He had not yet published anything in 1656, either for or against his religion. But Spinoza loved to talk. Apparently, he talked fast and well. What was worse, he discussed his subversive ideas with the gentiles. Two years after Spinoza's *herem*, an Augustinian monk named Tomás Soblano y Robles informed the Inquisition in Madrid about his trip to Amsterdam, where he had met Dr. Prado and Spinoza. They had told him that they had been observant Jews but had changed their minds because they didn't believe that Jewish law was true, or that souls were immortal, or that God was anything more than a philosophical idea. If

Spinoza said this to a Spanish monk, he certainly would have shared these thoughts with a more sympathetic audience of Collegiants and Mennonites.

Spinoza is said to have written an apologia to justify his actions after his ban. We don't know if this is true, or what it might have contained, but he began to think about his *Short Treatise on God, Man, and His Well-Being* (Korte verhandeling van God, de mensch en deszelvs welstand) soon after the *herem*. His ideas on the nature of God, the various ways of attaining knowledge, and his definition of freedom are already laid out in this early work, written around 1660. Much of this would be refined in later books, culminating in *Ethics*, published after his death. God, he wrote in the *Short Treatise*, is the only infinite substance, from which all finite things emanate, and "in God's infinite intellect no substance can be more perfect than that which already exists in Nature."[9] Substance exists independently from anything else. He had not yet used the phrase "God or nature," as though they were the same thing, but that was the implication. God was not like some wise, moral, or majestic creator of the world; he was an active force of nature present in everything, and always had been, and always would be.

Spinoza's definitions of freedom and happiness, which would run through all his books, are already substantially worked out in the *Short Treatise*, which means he must have been preparing these ideas well before he was banned from the synagogue. A thinking human being can be free by "directly uniting his intellect with God"—that is, with nature. This allows a person to conceive ideas that are not simply derived from others, from hearsay, or gossip, or prejudice. Understanding nature, logically, scientifically, and sometimes instinctively, can only come from unfettered and autonomous thought. As he puts it in the *Treatise on the Emendation of the Intellect*, written before the *Short Treatise*, we must learn to understand nature through the study of mechanics and other sciences, but above all by "finding a way to heal our minds, as much as we can, to purify our minds so we can understand things as well as possible without being led astray."[10]

This is why Spinoza has often been called the father of scientific thought. But he always equated the understanding of nature, or the love of God through the intellect, with happiness, even pleasure. Certainly, unbridled passions can enslave us, impede clear thinking, and muddy our understanding. But he was never a scold. His idea of perfection and freedom had nothing to do with repenting for our sins with sacrifice, self-denial, or any such thing. Christian puritanism was far from his conception of the good. "Knowledge of good and evil," he would later write in his *Ethics*, "is nothing but an idea of joy and sadness,"[11] and "a desire that arises from Joy is stronger, other things equal, than one that arises from Sadness."[12]

Spinoza didn't, however, need to be lewd or mocking to upset the religious, whether they be Jewish or Christian. His insistence on thinking freely for himself, without the mediation of clerics or clouding his mind with angels, saints, or other miraculous or supernatural notions, and his idea of God as the infinite substance of nature, rather than a divine creator, was a direct challenge to everything for which the pastors, priests, and rabbis stood. Which is why the rabbis advised the *ma'amad* to "cancel" him before he could do more damage. And Spinoza was well aware of how much damage the clerics of whatever denomination could do to him. In a letter to his Anglo-German friend Henry Oldenburg, written in 1662, a letter mostly about chemical experiments, he wrote about finishing his short book *Treatise on the Emendation of the Intellect*. He had no firm plan to publish it yet, "Since I fear, of course, that the theologians of our time may be offended and with their usual hatred attack me, who absolutely dreads quarrels."[13]

Dr. Prado and others who had been landed with a *herem* asked to be taken back, because they couldn't stand the isolation. Deprived of support from their community and unable to conduct business with other Jews, social isolation could also be financially ruinous. It made it almost impossible to make a living. This was a problem for Spinoza too, at least in the beginning, but he was never really isolated. He was rescued by his gentile friends: the Collegiants, the freethinkers who gathered at Jan Rieuwertsz's bookstore, the Mennonites and Socinianists whom Spinoza had met at the stock exchange, a few Quakers, and of course his Latin teacher, Franciscus van den Enden. Some of these friends, such as Simon Joosten de Vries, had more than enough money to keep their brilliant friend going.

It is hard to know what Spinoza's exact movements were between the *herem* and his move in 1661 to Rijnsburg, the village outside Leiden. Some believe he spent time at the home of a wealthy friend near Ouderkerk, where Spinoza's parents were buried. Then he might also have stayed at the country house of a rich judge, named Coenraad Burgh, whose son, Albert, was a friend of Spinoza's until he became a zealous Catholic convert in the 1670s and Spinoza got tired of arguing with him. But he was probably still living in Amsterdam, while going back and forth to Leiden to attend lectures at the university.

While in Amsterdam, Spinoza moved his parental bed into the bohemian household of Van den Enden, located on the Singel, one of the handsome but pungent canals that circumvented the city center. Baruch became Benedictus, meaning the same thing—namely, "Blessed"—and he acted in Van den Enden's plays, gave lessons in Hebrew, and helped his teacher's daughter, Clara Maria, instruct the younger students in lieu of paying rent. Life for Spinoza was never a party. He drank beer in moderation and ate frugally. In later life, he often subsisted on a diet of raisins and milk gruel. No heavy Dutch sausage and potato stews for him. People called him "Mr. Spinach," a vegetable that was supposed to nourish the human brain.[14]

There is no clear evidence of any amorous inclinations,

even though Clara Maria is said to have caught Spinoza's eye. Legend has it that his supposed rival for her affections, a medical student named Theodor Kerckring, won her over with an expensive pearl necklace. Johannes Colerus mentions that Spinoza had wanted to marry Clara Maria. Her age—thirteen in 1657—might not have been a barrier; a Jewish girl at the time would have been able to marry at the age of twelve. Then, of course, she was not Jewish, but Catholic. A better explanation for Spinoza's lifelong celibacy was his total commitment to individual autonomy and freedom. He was in favor of human happiness and saw love as an essential condition of joy and procreation. But he pointed out in his *Ethics* how easily love can turn to hate, because of sexual jealousy, or other external factors; the greater the love for someone, the more one will hate that person once passion cools. Spinoza, by choice or not, never took that risk.

He remained friendly with Kerckring, his supposed rival in love, who went on to become a medical doctor with a special interest in gynecology. Kerckring also stayed close to Van den Enden, and eventually did marry his daughter, possibly as a match of convenience. The wedding took place in 1671, the same year that Van den Enden left for France on his ill-fated mission to topple Louis XIV from his throne. The would-be revolutionary wanted to leave his daughter in the safe hands of a trusted former pupil.

Whether Van den Enden was the first person to introduce Spinoza to the ideas of Descartes is impossible to know. But he certainly enhanced his Cartesian education. No educated person could get around Descartes. A lifelong Catholic, Descartes had liberated Dutch minds by arguing that everything including Aristotelian notions of the soul should be tested by human reason. His main contribution was the idea that nature can be explained mechanically in terms of motion. The mind, separate from our bodies, is like "a ghost in the machine," in the words of Gilbert Ryle, the British philosopher.[15] Everything from the movement of the planets to human anatomy to ethics should be subjected to scientific, mathematical scrutiny. Doubt is the beginning of proper inquiry. Matter consists of moving particles and is devoid of soul. The earth, as Copernicus had already observed at a high price, revolves around the sun. Naturally, this kind of thinking, discussed with infectious enthusiasm in Van den Enden's dining room under paintings of Jesus Christ and of the princes of Orange, enraged the Calvinist clerics, and the Aristotelian professors who still dominated the Dutch academic world. Just as naturally, this inflamed the still simmering conflicts between the conservative, religious, Orangist factions of the republic and the more liberal regents and their supporters among the merchants of Amsterdam. De Witt's professors at Leiden University were Cartesians.

Indeed, some of Descartes's most implacable enemies in Dutch academia drew a direct line from the Cartesian threat to the old quarrels of the 1610s between the liberal Arminians and the orthodox Gomarists. Like the Remonstrant or Socinianist heresies, the ideas of Descartes, often misinterpreted, were considered a direct challenge to the authority of the church, and thus, to the unity of the Dutch Republic. One of his most ferocious opponents was a Calvinist theologian and rector of Utrecht University named Gysbert Voetius, who saw Cartesian skepticism as a recipe for atheism and moral collapse. There was a strong element of anti-papism in some of this criticism, as in Voetius's reference to the Jesuit founder Ignatius de Loyola, when he fulminated against those "who are imbued with Loyolitical Scepticism against the authority of the Bible."[16]

Voetius's quarrel with the Cartesians inflamed another row he initiated in the 1650s. In his view, the magistrates of the Dutch Republic were remiss in their duty to protect the Reformed Church. There was no difference of opinion among Calvinists that the magistrates were delegated by God to make sure that people kept to the right faith. The question was how far their remit stretched. Voetius and other conservatives thought that they were not doing enough to stamp out drinking, gambling, wearing long hair, theatrical performances, and disregarding the sabbath. A "Further Reformation" was badly needed. His opponent in this matter was a German-born theologian named Johannes Cocceius, who took a less doctrinal view of scripture and advocated "Christian liberty" instead of a more radical Reformation. *Gedogen* was his preferred approach to human foibles. Soon the church, as well as the universities, were divided between Voetians and Cocceians.

These fights, and the conflicts over Descartes, were so furious that Calvinists worried about another schism in their church. This didn't happen, but many university professors, as well as some of the regents, had been influenced by Descartes's "new philosophy" and were shaking the Aristotelian foundations of philosophy. As is so often the case—not only in the middle of the seventeenth century—the real bone of contention was the question of political authority. Who should be in control of higher education? Should the church have any say over academic appointments? Who should prevail in academic disputes—the theologians or the philosophers? Fierce rows over these issues erupted in Utrecht and Leiden, involving professors and students. A debate between a Cartesian and an anti-Cartesian professor at Leiden in 1647 drew such a huge crowd that their "heads reached to the vault."[17] People climbed over tables to hear every word of arguments about free will and God's grace. It was a most peculiar debate, because even mentioning the name of Descartes was considered inflammatory; his ideas could only be discussed as though they came from thin air.

In 1656, the year of Spinoza's *herem*, things had come to such a head that the state council of Holland made professors of philosophy promise, "for the sake of peace and calm," to "cease propounding the philosophical principles drawn from Descartes' philosophy, which today gives offense to a number of people."[18] This might seem a strange demand in a republic that prided itself on following the principles of True Freedom. In fact, it was part of a typically Dutch compromise. De Witt, on the advice of some Cartesian professors, decided on a formula that would protect the freedom to philosophize, while ostensibly answering the concerns of orthodox Calvinists. Professors had to swear not to use their freedom "to the detriment of theology and holy scripture."[19] The solution was to separate philosophy from theology, and to keep philosophy clear from metaphysics. Even though Descartes could not be named in public, his ideas were not only tolerated, but widely disseminated, and prominent Cartesians were given prestigious chairs at the major universities. Once again, something officially forbidden was *gedoogd*. If this was hypocrisy, it was a necessary hypocrisy to keep orthodoxy and dogmatism from crushing the freedom to think.

Spinoza would later write about this very thing in his *Theological-Political Treatise*, where he argued for the clean partition of philosophy and theology. The Bible teaches people only piety, and to "want to accommodate it to philosophy" is to "ascribe to the Prophets many things they did not think of even in their dreams." However, to make "reason and Philosophy the handmaiden of Theology" is to accept ancient prejudices as God's truth, which would destroy our capacity to think. To confuse the two things, "one with reason, and the other without," is folly.[20]

Still, not only was Descartes himself a religious man, but so were many of his most ardent supporters. One was a theologian named Abraham Heidanus. An inspiring teacher and adventurous thinker, Heidanus remained an orthodox Calvinist who tried to link Descartes's ideas about human will to God's grace—which was a tall order, but not impossible. Not the human will, as in Descartes, but God's grace allows humans to reach for the truth through rational thought. Then there was Adriaan Heereboord, a professor of logic at Leiden University. Heereboord defended Descartes as a "hero," whose method of doubt and scientific inquiry had helped thinkers recover the "invaluable liberty of the mind."[21] The point of philosophy, in Heereboord's view, was not to follow the word of this or that sage, but to study "God and Nature, the Macrocosm as well as the Microcosm."[22] Two other professors injected Cartesian ideas into their lectures: a Flemish Catholic who converted to Calvinism named Arnold Geulincx, and a philosopher who taught medicine named Johannes de Raey.

If Spinoza spent time auditing philosophy classes in Leiden while still living with Van den Enden in Amsterdam, which seems likely, he might not have come across Heereboord, whose heavy drinking had brought his academic career to a sad end, but he might well have studied with the others. Only in his twenties, Spinoza already had a solid grounding in the classics of Rome and Greece, in mathematics, astronomy, anatomy, physics, chemistry, the ideas of Bacon, Hobbes, Machiavelli, and especially Descartes, but what made him unique among his peers was his knowledge of Jewish philosophy. Some of his learning was imbibed at the yeshiva, some at Van den Enden's place, some at the bookstores and private meetings of freethinkers in Amsterdam, and some most probably in Leiden. Several men who studied at Leiden at the same time became his closest friends.

One of them, Lodewijk Meijer, was probably at Spinoza's bedside when he died. It was Meijer who helped Spinoza get his *Principles of Cartesian Philosophy* (Principia philosophiae cartesianae) published in 1663, and not only translated the text into Dutch but wrote an introduction. A rare non-Mennonite among Spinoza's friends, Meijer was born into a family of Lutherans. Apart from his medical studies, Meijer was a great lover of the theater, like Van den Enden, in whose productions he doubtless took part. Later on, he became the director of the Amsterdam Municipal Theater. While still a student, he wrote a poetic account of *Medea*, featuring Maria Clara's sister Adriana Clementia in the title role. She was only fifteen at the time, which seems a trifle young for the role, but outraged Calvinist preachers would have objected to the spectacle whatever the age of the actress.

Meijer was advanced in his thinking. His aim was to approach "God's truth" through Cartesian rationalism. His book *Philosophy as the Interpreter of Holy Scripture* (Philosophia S. scripturae interpres) (1666) was denounced by the Reformed Church as a godless and blasphemous work. Another, perhaps even more radical friend from the Leiden days was Adriaan Koerbagh. He studied medicine and law in Utrecht, as well as Leiden, where he became an enthusiastic Cartesian who would follow in Spinoza's radical footsteps. Alas for him, he decided to publish his scandalous thesis that reason was the source of happiness only in Dutch, which resulted in his sticky end in prison, where he was punished for dipping his pen in "the ink of hell."[23]

Clearly, then, Spinoza cast out of his community, was never alone. Not even all Jews dodged his company. He continued seeing Dr. Prado, at least until the doctor tried desperately and unwisely to undo his last *herem* by attacking Rabbi Morteira, whereupon he was forced to move to Antwerp, where he died a pauper after attempting to become a Christian again, apparently without success.

Meanwhile, Spinoza had to find a way to make a living, even though he could count on financial support from his wealthy friends. Colerus heard from Spinoza's last landlord that he made a little money sketching portraits of friends in ink and charcoal. Apparently, they were not bad. Even so, he didn't pursue this as a calling. That he chose to grind lenses was neither incidental nor without meaning. His interest was scientific, as much as practical. In a way, the art of cutting and polishing glass to see more clearly, the macrocosm as well as the microcosm, in Professor Heereboord's words, was analogous to Spinoza's aim to purify the mind to think more clearly. Many great thinkers of the time were interested in grinding glass and making microscopes and telescopes, including Descartes himself. From the beginning of his stay in the Dutch Republic, Descartes had wanted to test his theories on light, optics, and refraction in practice by constructing a machine for grinding lenses. He tried to entice a famous lens grinder in Paris named Jean Ferrier to join him in the icy northern province of Friesland, where he was teaching at the University of Franeker. It would be uncomfortable, he wrote to Ferrier, and hard work, but in a year, he promised, "I would dare hope that we would see, by your means, whether there are animals on the moon."[24]

Seeing more clearly was central to the great paintings of the Dutch Golden Age. Whether or not Vermeer used lenses and mirrors to paint sharper images in more detail, as some people insist, he was obsessed with light in all its different qualities. Light already had the connotation of Enlightenment long before this became the name of a philosophical movement, and Goethe supposedly asked for more light on his deathbed. Light was used in a moral sense, a way to illuminate the darkness of religious obscurantism or moral turpitude. In 1668 Adriaan Koerbagh, Spinoza's friend who would get into such serious trouble, wrote an anti-Christian tract, which was swiftly pulped, entitled *A Light Shining in Dark Places: To Illuminate the Main Questions of Theology and Religion* (Schrijvende in duystere plaatsen: Om te verligten de voornaamste zaken der Gods geleertheyd en Gods dienst). Spinoza's great Mennonite friend Pieter Balling wrote a pamphlet in 1662 in which he proposed a solution to sectarian strife and religious intolerance. If only, he argued, people would follow their "inner Light," or "the light of truth."[25]

Antonie van Leeuwenhoek, born in the same year as Spinoza, became world famous for his microscopic examination of microbes. Christiaan Huygens, the patrician scholar who would become Spinoza's friend, had by the time of the latter's *herem* already invented the pendulum clock and discovered Saturn's rings. When Spinoza was following lectures at Leiden, Huygens was there working on Descartes's theories about light. But Spinoza didn't need to go to Leiden to find a teacher. One of the extraordinary men in Van den Enden's circle was a Flemish Mennonite named Jan Glazemaker. In the late 1650s, he was already well known as the translator of Livy, Homer, Erasmus, and Descartes. As his name indicates, he also ground glass. That had been his father's trade, and he continued in his footsteps. Glazemaker was to be one of Spinoza's most loyal supporters. He offered to translate one of Spinoza's books from Latin into Dutch as well, but Spinoza, fearing too much exposure, put a stop to that.

With so many good friends, one wonders why Spinoza chose to leave the stimulation of one of the most exciting cities of Europe and settle in a village outside Leiden. Perhaps Amsterdam was too stimulating, and he wanted a quiet place to start writing in earnest. Another possible reason might have been that Rabbi Morteira couldn't abide the presence of his renegade pupil in the same city. Spinoza hadn't been banned for nothing. Moving around in perfect freedom, spreading his noxious ideas, he was a menace not only to Jews, but to all good citizens. Claims have been made that the municipal authorities were pressured by the rabbi to get Spinoza out of Amsterdam. There is no evidence of this. But they would not have acted on such entreaties anyway. Spinoza was *gedoogd*. He only left Amsterdam in 1661, by which time his rabbinical nemesis had died.

6

Far from the Madding Crowd

THE VILLAGE OF RIJNSBURG isn't much to speak of now. It was even quieter when Spinoza moved there by boat from Amsterdam in the summer of 1661. He wouldn't have had much luggage, apart from the parental bed, which had to be dismantled for transport, and his lens-grinding tools. The redbrick house he moved into was simple, but certainly not a pauper's dwelling. There was enough room on the ground floor for a wooden table, a small bookcase, a spot to grind his lenses, and a desk on which to write. Spinoza had one room for his work, and one for eating and sleeping. Winters would have been cold and damp, which can't have helped his weak lungs, quite apart from the noxious effects of breathing glass particles while at work on his lenses.

His diet was as frugal as always. Colerus tells us that he ate mostly gruel with butter, sometimes with a glass of beer. A receipt found in his papers showed that he only drank two half pints of wine in a whole month. Friendly invitations to share more copious dinners in Leiden, The Hague, or Amsterdam, when he visited to see old and new friends, were usually turned down.

Why did Spinoza choose Rijnsburg, of all places to settle? The vicinity of Leiden University must have been one attraction. Another was that this rural spot had been a refuge for Mennonites, Remonstrants, Arminians, Socinianists, and other Christian "Collegiants," who would meet there twice a year to pray and discuss matters of common interest, often to do with the moral improvement of society. Spinoza's landlord, Herman Homan, who had built his house in Rijnsburg as a country retreat to find peace and quiet as well as safety in times of plague, was himself connected to the Collegiants. Perhaps Spinoza was referred to him by a freethinking patrician in Amsterdam named Koenraad van Beuningen, who later became mayor of the city and director of the Dutch East India Company. Since many of the Collegiants were from the regent class, they have been described as forerunners of what socialists would later call bourgeois liberalism. To think of Spinoza, whose ideas were so radical, as a bourgeois liberal might seem strange, but it is not far off the mark; his ideas were daring, but he was always suspicious of too much zeal.

The Collegiants of Rijnsburg began as a small community of Remonstrants in a neighboring village who saw themselves as heirs to the apostolic tradition. At their regular meetings, monthly at first, later every six months, they would take turns to interpret the scripture. Their free-spirited discussions attracted liberal intellectuals from the larger cities, some of whom would move from arguments about God to scientific inquiries about nature. Theology was replaced more and more by philosophy— that is, by science. But their rationalism still had a strong ethical purpose; they were all strong believers in the ideals expressed in Christ's Sermon on the Mount. By the time Spinoza had settled into his two rooms in Homan's house, his still unpublished ideas were avidly discussed among the Collegiants of Amsterdam, many of whom were his friends, such as Jarig Jellesz, Simon Joosten de Vries, and Pieter Balling. They were frequent guests of Spinoza in Rijnsburg as well, sometimes too frequent for his taste.

Before Spinoza's move to Rijnsburg, the Amsterdam Collegiants had also welcomed English Quakers in their midst. Quakers had begun to arrive in Holland in large numbers to escape persecution in England. In 1656 a traveling Quaker evangelist named James Nayler caused a scandal by riding into Bristol on a white horse on Palm Sunday, crying, "Holy! Holy! God of Israel!" For this eccentric behavior, he was arrested, had his tongue pierced with hot iron, and the letter *B* for *blasphemy* branded on his forehead.

The Quakers had a particular interest in the Jews of Amsterdam, because they believed that the messiah's second coming was at hand, but not before Jews repented for their errors and became Christians. To speed things up, Quakers sought Jews out in their homes and the synagogue to show them the correct way to salvation. A man named William Ames wanted to distribute pamphlets written by Margaret Fell Fox, also known as the Mother of the Quakers. One of them was titled *For Manasseth Ben Israel. The Call of the Jewes out of Babylon. Which is good tidings to the Meek, Liberty to the Captives, and for the opening of the Prison Doores* (1656). Another was called *A Loving Salutation to The seed of Abraham among the Jewes: where ever they are scattered up and down upon the face of the earth* (1656). To find a wider audience among the Jews, the Quakers thought it might be a good idea to have these writings translated into Hebrew as well as Dutch. Extraordinary as it might seem, their chosen translator most probably was Spinoza. In 1657 a leading Quaker in Amsterdam named William Caton wrote to Fell Fox: "I have been with a Jew and have shewed him they book & have asked him what languadge would be the fittest for them he told me

Portugees or Hebrew, for if it were Hebrew they might understand it at Jerusalem or in almost any other place of the world; And he hath undertaken to translate it for us, he being expert in several Languadges."[1] That this Jew is likely to have been Spinoza is confirmed by a letter from Ames, written to Fell Fox in the same year, in which he says, "There is a Jew at Amsterdam that by the Jews is Cast out. . . . I gave order that one of the duch Copyes of thy book should be given toe him and he sent me word he would Come toe oure meeting."[2]

Spinoza might have undertaken the task because he needed the money. Perhaps he was also curious to know what these English dissenters had to say, and some of what they said would have had his sympathy. A Quaker preacher named Samuel Fisher, who was regularly locked up in prisons in England and France for spreading unwelcome ideas, was the author of some remarkable books with such titles as *One Antidote more against that provoking Sin of Swearing* (1660) and *Anti-Sacerdotism the deep dotage of the D. D. Divines Discovered* (1653). This may seem to denote a different intellectual universe from the one Spinoza was used to. But in fact, Fisher's view that the Pentateuch couldn't have been written by Moses, and that the words in the Bible cannot have come straight from God's sacred lips, but were surely written by a variety of men, would have struck a chord. Steven Nadler, in whose book I found this information, thinks it is possible that "many of Spinoza's own radical ideas on the authorship and redaction of Scriptures found reinforcement— or even their origin—in discussions he had with Fisher and other Quakers in 1657."[3]

This is indeed possible, although Spinoza may already have come to such conclusions before Ames and others came to spread their millenarian message in Holland. Might Spinoza have sought the company of Quakers and Rijnsburg Collegiants because he was spiritually homeless, and needed some kind of religious consolation? Anything is possible, but this doesn't seem very likely.

There is no evidence that conversion to Christianity in any form ever tempted him, despite what some people claimed at the time. A Danish traveler named Olaus Borch wrote in his diary on May 17, 1661, that "there were certain atheists in Amsterdam, most of them Cartesians, among which an impudent atheist Jew." Later, the same tourist heard that "here in the village Rijnsburg lived somebody who had become a Christian from a Jew and now was nearly an atheist." He added, however, that this Jew, now a Christian, "lives without doing any harm to other people; and he occupies himself with the construction of telescopes and microscopes."[4] In fact, while polishing lenses, which friends would come and pick up periodically to sell for him, Spinoza was already working on the outline of *Ethics*, his analysis of God, human passions, and concepts of freedom, as well as finishing his *Short Treatise on God, Man, and His Well-Being*.

There has been much debate about the form of the *Short Treatise* and how it came to be written. One claim is that Spinoza never wrote the book at all, but that his friends stitched together a compilation of his notes and thoughts. Since Spinoza told his friend Henry Oldenburg in a letter in 1662 that he was working on the book, this seems questionable. He also asks Oldenburg's advice on the wisdom of publishing such a book, given the hostile reception he anticipated from Calvinist preachers. Oldenburg replies that he would love to see the book published. After all, he writes, "Your Republic is very free, and gives great freedom for philosophizing. And your own prudence will suggest to you that you express your concepts and your opinion as moderately as possible. For the rest, leave the outcome to fate."[5]

Oldenburg was being a little naïve, perhaps, since it was the nature of Spinoza's ideas and not the mode of their expression that was the issue. Oldenburg was an important man in Spinoza's life, even though they only met in person once, in Rijnsburg, just after Spinoza had moved there. The son of a philosopher in Bremen, Oldenburg was born in 1617 and studied theology. He had spent time in the Dutch Republic and in England, where he was a private teacher to noble families and later, in the 1640s, a diplomat at Cromwell's court. A sophisticated German polyglot, Oldenburg not only knew Latin and Greek, of course, but also French, Dutch, Italian, and English. He moved in the best circles, making friends with Thomas Hobbes and John Milton, and finding a patron in the great chemist Robert Boyle. Queen Christina of Sweden, the enlightened monarch who employed Descartes as her instructor in philosophy and sponsored many freethinkers and libertines, gave Oldenburg a stipendium. In 1660 this learned gentleman who, according to Milton, spoke English more accurately and fluently than any foreigner he had ever known, was one of the founding members of the Royal Society, and later its secretary. He married well into the English upper class and owned a fine property in the country. It speaks for Spinoza's reputation that this cosmopolitan grandee would seek him out in Rijnsburg before Spinoza had even published his first book.

The meeting was evidently a great success. They spoke for hours in Spinoza's tiny room about God, nature, the sciences, Descartes, Bacon, and more. Oldenburg also shared with Spinoza an interest in optics. After he had returned to England, he wrote that he had found it hard to tear himself away from Spinoza's company: "Knowledge of things of enduring importance, combined with kindness and graciousness (all of which Nature and your own Diligence have most abundantly enriched you with), have in them such charms that they must win for themselves the love of any honorable man, educated as becomes a free man."[6] The highborn pretentions of these words might have appealed to Spinoza's Spanish side. In any case, he told Oldenburg how much he also prized his friendship. Thinking of his new friend's many qualities, Spinoza felt honored "to enter into the close friendship you continue to offer me and deign to ask of me to return. I shall take great care to cultivate it zealously."[7]

Spinoza had good reason to be cautious about publishing, for his ideas were more explosive than even Oldenburg quite realized. Oldenburg wanted to know how Spinoza could be so sure that God can be defined as the one perfect, infinite substance, of which all other things that can be seen, measured, felt, heard, or thought are modes. After all, Oldenburg wrote, definitions contain only concepts in our minds, and our minds can conceive many things that don't exist, so he fails to see how he "can infer God's existence from my concept of him."[8]

Spinoza's reply is slightly testy and offers a perhaps not entirely convincing explanation. He denies saying that the existence of just *anything* follows from its definition, but only of something "that is conceived through itself and in itself." There is only one substance. That is what Spinoza means by God, or nature, which is a self-creating, infinite, self-perpetuating force. What can be perceived by humans are the modes of this single substance: finite things that are alive, as well as mental activities, such as thoughts, opinions, or theories. The laws of God/nature follow a logic that can be known in theory through human reason. Spinoza reminds Oldenburg that the difference between the knowledge of God or nature and other concepts should be evident to "a Philosopher, who is supposed to know the difference between a fiction and a clear and distinct concept."[9] Spinoza often used an example from geometry to drive this point home when he felt his interlocutors were being obtuse. When Spinoza was asked in a much later letter, from a Catholic convert, how he could be sure he had found the true philosophy, he answered that he understood "true philosophy" in the same way his friend knew that the sum of three angles of a triangle were equal to two right angles.[10]

He ends another letter to Oldenburg by telling his friend exactly why his book, if it were published, was bound to provoke the hateful rage of preachers. One thing, especially, was bound to make them angry: "I do not separate God from Nature as everyone known to me has done. So I look for your advice, regarding you as a most faithful friend whose honesty it would be wrong to doubt."[11]

Spinoza was right. What he had done was something very few of his contemporaries could follow, for he had severed God from any transcendence. Since God is self-causing, infinite, and eternal, God cannot by definition stand outside the world, any more than nature can. The entire universe *is* God. The activity of nature, what Samuel Taylor Coleridge called "nature in the active sense," is what Spinoza called "Natura Naturans."[12] Everything that comes about within nature through this causally active dimension is Natura Naturata. There is no room in this idea for any sacred notion of good and evil either, as God is morally indifferent; there is nothing that was handed down on tablets from heaven and the like. Good is merely a human notion that exists relative to evil, and the other way around. In Spinoza's words: "For one never says something is good except in respect to something that is not so good, or not so useful to us as something else."[13]

This was a remarkable and deeply subversive idea. Even the Deists, who shared Spinoza's view of God as indifferent, could not think of him as anything but a force acting upon and standing outside the world. Descartes certainly couldn't. This allowed rationalists to believe in science and take a mechanistic view of nature, while still believing in a transcendent God. As Stuart Hampshire observed, "It was convenient in scientific practice to regard the Universe as a giant clock-work mechanism, which, once wound up and set in motion by the Supreme Clock-maker in accordance with his design and laws of motion, revolved on its own (except perhaps for occasional interferences in the mechanism by the maker, called miracles)."[14] Spinoza had no time at all for miracles. If anything in nature seems mysterious to us, this is due to our lack of sufficient knowledge to understand it.

No wonder, then, that Spinoza wrote at the end of the *Short Treatise:* "Do not be surprised at these novelties, for you know very well that it is no obstacle to the truth of a thing that it is not accepted by many. And as you are also aware of the character of the age in which we live, I would ask you urgently to be very careful about communicating these things to others."[15]

A few close friends grasped Spinoza's ideas, even if they often expressed themselves in more conventional religious terms. Pieter Balling, for example, in his pamphlet entitled *Light on the Candlestick* (Het licht op den kandelaar), written in 1661, urged people to seek the "the Light of Truth" inside themselves. "Only light can conquer darkness, and only knowledge can dispel ignorance." Balling believed that the light of reason would enable us to understand things so clearly that there could no longer be any doubt: "Man can find certainty by knowing God to the extent that finite and limited beings can understand what is eternal and unlimited."[16] Even though Spinoza's idea of a critical examination of scripture didn't involve any kind of inner light, Balling, in his rather exalted prose, is describing what Spinoza called "substance," or God, or nature, whose laws can be known through reason. As a Dutch scholar of religion put it a hundred years ago: "The hands of [Balling] might feel like 'the law of Christ,' but the voice is Spinoza's." He added that in theological terms, "this was as far as a humanist-spiritualist heretic could go inside the Christian faith."[17]

Again, Spinoza never was inside the Christian faith, nor did he aspire to be. And he was no longer a religious Jew. So, was he an atheist? Pierre Bayle, for one, thought he was. He also believed, rather curiously, that Spinoza's atheism had something in common with "Oriental philosophies" in Japan and China. Curious, but not absurd. Other people have made similar claims, comparing Spinoza's calm reflection to Hindu or Buddhist prac-

tices. Knowledge of China trickling into Europe in the seventeenth century produced a problem for the Christian world. How
to explain a society where virtuous behavior was prized and
nurtured outside the Christian faith? This was baffling. Bayle
had only a superficial knowledge of Chinese and Japanese cultures and conflated vague notions of Buddhism with Confucian
thought. What he saw in Spinoza, however, was the same co-
nundrum that China conjured up in many European minds. Bayle
had to admit that everyone who knew Spinoza agreed that he
was "morally irreproachable." And yet this same man proposed
"the most monstrous hypothesis one can possibly imagine, the
most absurd, the most diametrically opposed to notions we hold
as most evident."[18] Obviously, then, Spinoza had to be a bit like
the Chinese.

Spinoza hated being accused of being an atheist and always
tried to defend himself against it. Perhaps he protested a little
too much because he was afraid of the consequences. His Marrano ancestors knew the smell of burning stakes only too well.
But I don't believe that caution was the only reason. What is
remarkable about his ripostes against accusations of atheism is
how closely they resemble the prejudices of Christian believers. Responding to the taunt of atheism in 1671 by a theologian
named Lambert van Velthuysen (who was a keen follower of
Descartes), Spinoza made several arguments. To the criticism
that he failed to grant freedom to God, he replied that, on the
contrary, God is entirely free, since everything necessarily flows
from God. He then made the following point: atheists are ex-
cessively interested in status and wealth, and he, Spinoza, could
never be accused of that. He was a humble man who never
chased after such unworthy goals, so how could he possibly be
an atheist? Knowing and loving God was his highest aim; all
worldly yearnings and desires were trivial in comparison. To be
a man of virtue, and treat others with justice and charity, was to
love God.[19]

Still, his God was far from the Christian, Jewish, Muslim, or indeed Chinese gods. His God did not reside in heaven and could not be conceived as anything but nature. And the eternal laws of this "divine nature" could be grasped by human intelligence. So, Spinoza loved God, as a rational thinker. In that sense, he was not an atheist. In every other sense, he was.

While Spinoza had ensconced himself in Rijnsburg to do his work and think in peace, he still went on regular trips to Amsterdam, to speak to his friends, and to Leiden, where he attended lectures with Adriaan Koerbagh and others, and he liked to watch a Danish anatomist named Niels Stensen (also known as Nicolas Steno) perform dissections. Friends, and sometimes curious strangers, would also come to visit him. Sometimes Rijnsburg attracted students from Leiden who liked to argue with the Collegiants. These occasions could get rowdy, and were unlikely to have been attended by Spinoza, who hated rowdiness. But some young men sought him out for private instruction. One of them was a student of theology named Johannes Casearius, a former Latin pupil of Van den Enden's, which is how Spinoza first came across him. They might even have left Amsterdam together. After a short stay in Leiden, Casearius moved in with Spinoza, as his private student in Cartesian philosophy.

Casearius's name first comes up in a letter to Spinoza from Simon Joosten de Vries, written in February 1663, informing Spinoza that his ideas were being avidly discussed among friends in Amsterdam, but that some things concerning the nature of substance and attributes were not yet entirely clear to them.[20] They were especially keen to sort out Spinoza's differences with Descartes. The letter then takes a more emotional turn. De Vries expresses his deep envy of Casearius, who is lucky enough to live with Spinoza under one roof, sharing his life from breakfast to dinner, and going for long walks, discussing weighty topics.

It is painful, writes De Vries, to be physically separated from Spinoza, but he assures him that his friend is always present in his mind. Oh, to be Casearius!

The tone of this letter, and possibly the fact that De Vries was a single man, has prompted speculation that his feelings for Spinoza were not just intellectual. Might he, or might Spinoza, or perhaps both, have been homosexual? Repressed, perhaps? Closeted? Possibly. But there is no evidence of this at all, apart from the longing expressed in De Vries's letter. To be sure, Spinoza shared his cherished bed with his live-in student, but that was unavoidable in such cramped quarters and not proof of any romantic attachment.

In any case, as Spinoza's reply to his Amsterdam friend clearly shows, Casearius was not a particularly welcome guest. Spinoza found him callow and annoying: "No one is more troublesome to me, and there is no one with whom I have to be more on my guard."[21]

Still, despite all his caution, Spinoza did get his first published book out of his tutelage of Caseaurius, namely *The Principles of Cartesian Philosophy*. He dictated the contents of this book to his student, setting out Descartes's principles, which the Frenchman had expressed in elegant prose, in the far less mellifluous form of geometric axioms. The Latin text was translated into Dutch by Pieter Balling, and an introduction was provided by Spinoza's other great friend, Dr. Lodewijk Meijer, who made it clear that Spinoza did not subscribe to all of Descartes's ideas. Meijer also stressed something close to Spinoza's heart, namely that the book was meant for an educated readership that wished to attain deeper insights than were within the grasp of "the common people." If dictators and hateful preachers were to be feared, then so was the unenlightened mob that would only be confused by ideas that were too hard for most people to grasp.

Despite Spinoza's wariness of his immature live-in student,

he does explain some of his main differences with Descartes in the book. Descartes believed in God as the great creator who set the clock of life in motion. Spinoza did not. Descartes thought that everything in heaven and earth must be doubted until proven true. This could mean that even God might sometimes play tricks on us. He said this despite being a religious man. Since Spinoza argued that everything came from one indivisible substance named God, without which nothing can exist, he thought that any hesitation about this matter was as ridiculous as doubting that the sum of three angles of a triangle were equal to two right angles.

Descartes famously had one unshakable conviction, however. He was a thinking being: "I think, therefore I am." Even if his thoughts were wrong, he was the one who was thinking them, so he had to exist. Another thing he believed was that God had a free will to do anything he liked, even change the laws of nature, if he wished, and that God had given humans a free will too, which was distinct from the human capacity to think. Since people have a free will, they are responsible for what they do, for better or worse. Spinoza disagreed. First, the laws of nature were not created on a divine whim. As Einstein would say: "God doesn't play dice with the universe." And "will" does not exist as an abstraction. Spinoza does not separate will from the intellect. There are individual acts of will, which are part of thinking. And thinking is a mode of that force called God or nature. Our thoughts are determined by an infinite number of causes, but they are not subject to some autonomous entity called free will. This doesn't make Spinoza's lifelong insistence on his freedom to think any less important. To "know God"—that is, to understand nature and our place in it—was the closest Spinoza came to offering a recipe for happiness.

Even though Spinoza did not pursue material luxury, sensual pleasure, status, or wealth, he was not unworldly, as several anecdotes of his earlier life in Amsterdam already suggest. He could be quite political when it helped to preserve or expand his freedom to think. In a letter to Oldenburg, sent in July 1663, Spinoza explained that he wrote *The Principles of Cartesian Philosophy* at the request of his Amsterdam friends. But he had high expectations that its publication would make "some highly placed people in my country wish to read other things I have written, expressing my own ideas this time. I hope they will make sure I can publish them without unpleasantness. . . . If not, I'd prefer to remain silent rather than to impose my ideas on people against the wishes of my country and make enemies of them."[22]

Exactly who these highly placed people were is not spelled out. Spinoza might have had Johan and Cornelis de Witt in mind, the two most powerful brothers in the land, or other prominent regents such as Koenraad van Beuningen, whom he knew personally. Alas, his wish to publish "other things" did not come true. His book on Descartes was the only one to appear during his lifetime bearing his name on the cover—the *Theological-Political Treatise* would be published anonymously in 1670 with a fake publisher's imprint. Jarig Jellesz paid for the publication of *The Principles*. And the publisher was Jan Rieuwertsz, the printer, publisher, and owner of the Book of Martyrs bookstore in Amsterdam. What Spinoza may not have foreseen was that his lectures on Descartes quickly made him a famous name all over Europe—the Europe, that is, of philosophers, scientists, and freethinkers, the "educated readership" favored by Pieter Balling in his introduction.

7

———◆·◆·◆———

Secular Salvation

ONE OF THE CURIOUS THINGS about the seventeenth century is that it was at once the heroic age of scientific speculation and the age of passionate religious millenarianism. The two tendencies could exist, sometimes even happily, side by side. Isaac Newton and Robert Boyle were no less prone to belief in the coming of a thousand-year paradise ruled by Jesus Christ and the saints than were millions of people without their intellectual distinction. English Puritans saw Oliver Cromwell as the messianic herald of this promised land. Quakers, Levelers, Ranters, and Diggers anxiously waited for apocalypse and the new millennium that would surely follow. So did many citizens of the Dutch Republic, constantly alert to divine signals of impending favors or punishment. The frequent outbreaks of the plague encouraged these spasms of hope and fear.

Some of the more prominent millenarians were well known to Spinoza. Rabbi Menasseh was a great believer in the messiah's imminent arrival, and he was often approached by Christian seekers who wished to be enlightened on the vital Jewish role in this happy event. One of the most peculiar figures in Spinoza's circle was a friend of Menasseh's named Petrus Serrarius (or Pierre Serrurier), who was born in London to a Huguenot family. Serrarius moved to Amsterdam in the 1630s, where he soon fell in with Quakers, Mennonites, and Collegiants. Exactly what Serrarius did for a living is mysterious, but he was an assiduous networker between London and Amsterdam, furnishing introductions here and acting as an intermediary there— between Spinoza and Henry Oldenburg, for example. He often functioned as Spinoza's international postman.

Serrarius was always on the lookout for omens. In 1662 a booklet published in the northern Dutch city of Groningen came to his attention, entitled *Something New and Miraculous* (Wat nieuws ende wonderlijk). He learned that in that year, the seven planets would come together in the sign of Sagittarius. This was the omen Serrarius had been waiting for. He wrote several pamphlets about the second coming of Christ, who would destroy godlessness and restore the kingdom of justice on earth.

Alas for Serrarius, this failed to happen. But God's punishment for man's sins could not have been clearer in the year that Spinoza moved from his rooms in Rijnsburg to new digs in the village of Voorburg, now a suburb of The Hague. The plague was devastating the country once more. A pamphlet was published in 1664 with the following text: "People will doubtless remember how God Almighty visited the city of Amsterdam with awful pestilence in 1663 and chastised us for considerable time with the same rod." By the end of that year, the pamphlet continues, 9,752 people had died in Amsterdam alone. In the beginning of 1664, "a terrible and swift fireball crossed the sky like a bullet with a long tail." After this horrific portent, "God's righteous anger" caused ever more people to die "in the fire of that dreadful disease."[1] Smoking vats of brimstone were placed in the streets to disinfect the air. Dogs, suspected of carrying the disease, were killed, while the rats were left untouched.[2] The streets of Amsterdam were so deserted that grass grew between the paving stones. Spinoza's brother Gabriel, like many people who could afford it, had left the plague-ridden city. He was bound for Barbados and its rich sugar plantations. And no sooner had Spinoza moved to Voorburg than he sought a refuge from the plague in a lovely country house on a river near Rotterdam, where the sister and brother-in-law of Spinoza's good friend Simon Joosten de Vries lived at the time.

The De Vries family had been touched by the black death. Simon's brother Frans and his wife, Sijtien, died in the summer of 1664. The body of his mother, Maria, was carried off soon after. Sadly, Pieter Balling, Spinoza's other close friend, lost his young son in 1663. He, too, had seen an augury of this tragic event. His correspondence with Spinoza throws an interesting light on the seventeenth-century culture of omens, portents, and prophesies, and Spinoza's response to such phenomena.

Balling said he had been half asleep when he heard his son, still in good health, gasping as though at death's door. This surely was a sign of what would come. Spinoza replies that his friend must have imagined it. Surely, the gasps were more vivid in his imagination than it sounded once he was fully conscious. Spinoza compared his friend's experience to one of his own. He woke up one morning from a dream about a scurvy black Brazilian. He continued to see the black man for some time as though he were real, until the image gradually faded away. This, he said, was analogous to Balling's story of hearing his son's agony. But there was an important difference. The reasons for these imaginary events were not the same. In the case of Spinoza's Brazilian, there was no question of a portent; in the case of Balling's son, there may have been.

Spinoza explains this as follows. We know that fevers in the body can result in delirious visions. We also know that our imagination is determined by our state of mind. The imagination follows the same steps as the intellect. It puts images and sensations in order, just as the intellect finds ways to connect things that can be proven. We cannot understand anything without our imagination coming up with a representation. Therefore, Spinoza continues, "there can be no question of omens if the imagination is stirred by physical causes, since such causes have nothing to do with anything happening in the future." But if what we imagine comes from our state of mind, this could be an omen, since "the mind can have a vague intimation of something yet to happen." Balling's love for his son was so intense that he became "part of his son." The soul of father and son have merged to the extent that the father can imagine what might happen to the child in the near future.[3]

Spinoza's letter is dated July 20, 1664. Since he mentions spending the last winter in Rijnsburg, despite already having moved to his new place in Voorburg by then, the letter could possibly have been written earlier. In any case, what is fascinating is Spinoza's empathy with his friend, who was soon to die of the plague himself, and his acute psychological insight. Whether Spinoza really believed in bad omens, or was trying to humor his friend, is impossible to know. But his philosophical ideas about the interaction of body and mind, and of the intellect and the imagination, are not just abstract speculations. Spinoza always had clear ideas about the practical use of philosophizing, in politics and human psychology. The goal was never just the accumulation of knowledge for its own sake, but to find a way to help people lead better, freer, happier lives. He was never detached from the world, or the people living in it.

If Spinoza had moved away from the distractions of Rijnsburg, where he was bothered by tiresome students from Leiden, in the hope of finding a quieter life in Voorburg, he had to have been disappointed. For he quickly fell into a very unpleasant local row, and the political omens for the Dutch Republic, threatened by a new war with England, were not good either. The local spat, as was so often the case, involved the appointment of a clergyman. Spinoza moved his bed, his books, and his lens-grinder into a simple two-story house—still there today—belonging to a middle-aged master painter named Daniël Tydeman and his wife, Margarita. Tydeman, although a member of the Reformed Church, was close to the Collegiants, which might explain how Spinoza got to know him. Because the preacher at Tydeman's church in Voorburg had moved on, or perhaps died, a new one had to be appointed. Tydeman was in favor of a relatively liberal-minded pastor. A request was sent to the local authorities who had to decide on these matters. This greatly upset the more orthodox members of the community, who asked for a preacher more to their liking. They attacked Tydeman and his friends for "acting out of pure malice." Worse than that, Tydeman had taken "an Amsterdammer named Spinosa, born of Jewish parents" as a lodger. This man was reputed to be "an atheist who mocks all religions and is a pernicious element in this republic, as many learned men and preachers who know him can attest."[4] And this dangerous atheist, they claimed, had been the author of Tydeman's request for an objectionable and unorthodox pastor.

It seems highly unlikely that Spinoza would have been directly involved in the appointment of a Calvinist preacher. If anything, the row was a mild version of the kind of sectarian conflict, whipped up by people with more fervor than sense, that he abhorred. He would have much preferred to be left alone to work on his lenses, his books, and possibly his sketches. Colerus claims to have seen drawings by Spinoza, one of which represented a dashing Italian fisherman who bore a remarkable resemblance to Spinoza himself. We must take Colerus's word for it, since such a picture has never been recovered.

The world outside Voorburg, with its petty quarrels over the appointment of clergymen, was in much deeper trouble.

Charles II had been restored to the English throne, and his government was hostile to the Dutch Republic. At issue was maritime supremacy, as well as royal aversion to republicanism. Dutch ships were raided on the high seas, and overseas possessions were taken over. In 1664 the English captured New Amsterdam and renamed it New York, after the duke of York, brother of King Charles. In March of the following year, England declared war on the republic. Walking to his office in The Hague, Johan de Witt could supposedly hear the canon blasts from the Battle of Lowestoft, which ended in a bad defeat for the Dutch navy. What made the Anglo-Dutch conflict ominous for De Witt was that King Charles and his diplomats in The Hague were conspiring with young Prince William of Orange and his followers to topple the True Freedom government and bring back the stadtholder. The old tensions between liberal regents and Orangists were being deliberately stirred up. And while the Dutch were at war with England, Louis XIV of France, no less of an enemy of the republic, was threatening an invasion from the south. The worse the threats, the more people called for an Orange stadtholder to save their country. Rule by the regents was put under severe pressure.

Harassed by the orthodox burghers in Voorburg, and quite aware of the dangers to a state that still provided a degree of freedom to intellectuals like himself, Spinoza worked hard on his two most famous works, *Ethics* and the *Theological-Political Treatise*. Being called a dangerous atheist only acted as a spur.

Spinoza had been spending some time in Amsterdam in 1665, seeing friends and working on the publication of his book about Descartes. Soon after returning to Voorburg he wrote a letter to his friend Johannes Bouwmeester, mentioning his fragile state of health. Spinoza had been suffering from a high fever, which persisted despite opening his vein for some bloodletting. He also mentions the Anglo-Dutch War, very much in the spirit of a Dutch patriot. There is "a great deal of talk," he writes, "about the English affairs, though nothing is certain. People expect the worst. The situation must be critical." So why, Spinoza wonders, "can't the navy be given free rein?" He fears that his "compatriots are trying to be too wise and too cautious." The facts will point the way in the end: "May heaven help us."[5]

The war comes up again in a letter to Oldenburg, his Anglo-German friend in London. The tone is more personally defiant than patriotic. In fact, Oldenburg, as an Anglophile member of the landed gentry, was on the English side, which didn't save him from being locked up for a short while after the war in the Tower of London under suspicion of revealing state secrets to foreigners; he had corresponded on philosophical matters with a friend in France, prompting Samuel Pepys to note in his diary that it is "very unsafe at this time to write, or almost do anything."[6] Spinoza is pleased to hear that the philosophers in England are well, and "not forgetting their task as members of the republic of science." War is absurd, he writes, but "these troubles don't make me laugh or cry. Instead, they encourage me to philosophize and to better observe human nature." He then explains three reasons why he is writing a treatise on the scripture. He wants to debunk the prejudices of theologians, for doing so would free the minds of sensible people to philosophize. Secondly, he wants to counter as much as he can the popular view of him as an atheist. Finally, he is adamant to stand up for the "freedom of philosophizing and saying what we think, which I want to defend in every way; here the preachers suppress it as much as they can with their excessive authority and aggressiveness."[7]

Spinoza's biblical criticism and views on religion were so bold that they could not be published in his lifetime, or at least not under his own name, even in the republic under Johan de Witt. *Ethics* is hard to read, since it is written as a sequence of propositions and proofs, as in Euclidian geometry. This book, which Spinoza wrote in fits and starts, was meant for serious philosophers. Drafts of *Ethics* were being passed around among friends as early as 1665. But it wasn't published in Holland until after Spinoza died in 1677. The *Theological-Political Treatise* is easier to read and was aimed at a wider audience of educated citizens ("sensible people")—regents, of course, but also the more open-minded Protestant clergy and their flock.

The masses, or *vulgus*, who could "no more be freed from their superstitions than from their fears," were not included by Spinoza. He wrote: "I don't ask the common people to read these things, nor anyone else who is struggling with the same effects as the common people. Indeed, I would prefer them to neglect this book entirely, rather than make trouble by interpreting it perversely, as they usually do with everything."[8]

Even so, the *Treatise* could only be published in Latin in 1670, without Spinoza's name, and with a fake imprint, to save the ever-loyal publisher Jan Rieuwertsz from getting into trouble. Plans for a Dutch translation were quickly scotched by Spinoza himself. He worried that a Dutch version would lead to a ban on the Latin text as well. The book only appeared in Dutch in 1693, in English in 1689, and in German in 1806.

Even in the 1660s, the claim that the Bible was the work of humans, that miracles were imaginary, and that clerics used religion to control the masses was hardly unique. Thomas Hobbes, whose *On the Citizen* (De cive) was published in Holland in 1647, and whose *Leviathan* was available in Dutch in 1667, said all these things, and was accused of being an atheist, like Spinoza, who probably read his work while writing his own *Treatise*. Hobbes called priests and pastors "a confederacy of deceivers, that, to obtain dominion over men in this present world, endeavor by dark and erroneous doctrines to extinguish within them the light, both of nature and of the gospel, and so to disprepare them for the kingdom of God to come."[9] Hobbes also noted that people no longer regard natural phenomena, such as rainbows, as miracles once they understand the natural causes.

But Spinoza, despite all his effort to be cautious, put forth these ideas with less circumspection and more clarity. Spinoza would not have spoken of a "kingdom of God to come." And while Hobbes was careful not to rule out the hand of God in wondrous events, Spinoza dismissed any notion of supernatural agency. This prompted Hobbes's remark that Spinoza had "outthrown" him, since he, Hobbes, "durst not write so boldly."[10]

The point of Spinoza's biblical criticism, showing how different parts of the scriptures were written at different times, by different people, and that the Pentateuch could not have been the work of Moses but of someone who lived much later, was not to dismiss the practical use of religion. His purpose was not to advocate the abolition of religious faith, but to separate scientific truth, established by rational means, from theology. He saw no point in trying to use reason to justify obscure or contradictory passages in the Bible. One neither could nor should expect religious texts to be rational. When Spinoza denounced the folly of trying to demonstrate the authority of scriptures with mathematical proofs, he might have been thinking of Maimonides, the twelfth-century Jewish philosopher, or perhaps Descartes, or perhaps also his friend, Dr. Lodewijk Meijer, whose rationalist interpretation of the Bible had gotten him into hot water with Calvinist authorities. For the authority of scriptures depended upon the authority of the prophets. And that authority was impervious to rational discourse. So long as people were free to philosophize, others should be free to believe anything they wished, provided their beliefs did no harm to others. There was no reason at all for the freedom to think rationally and religious faith to be in each other's way. "Separating belief from philosophy," he wrote, "was the main purpose of this whole work."[11]

Still, even though Spinoza thought that religion was fine, so long as it made people behave decently, he was a fierce critic of clerics whose sectarian fanaticism crushed the freedom to think and disturbed the social order with endless and often bloody conflicts. (The Thirty-Years' War, pitting Protestant against Catholic powers, and leaving up to eight million people dead, had only ended two decades before.) One interesting aspect of the chapters on religion in the *Treatise* is how much harder Spinoza is on Judaism than on Christianity, even though the Reformed preachers were far more formidable enemies of free speech and thought in the Dutch Republic than the rabbis ever could hope to be. Attacking the Reformed would, of course, have been a much riskier enterprise than upsetting the conservative rabbis.

If Rabbi Morteira was furious with Spinoza's defiance of the Jewish laws before, he would have been outraged by the *Treatise* if he had lived to read it. Spinoza attacks all the sacred tenets of Judaism. Not only were the Mosaic laws not written by God, but they were redundant. The ancient Hebrew people had been lucky to live for a time in a relatively prosperous society governed by just laws, revealed by Moses. The Hebrew nation "was not chosen by God before others because of its intellect or its peace of mind, but because of its social order and the fortune by which it came to have a state, and kept it for so many years."[12] Apart from that, nothing distinguished the Jews from other people. Virtue and intelligence, and the knowledge/love of God/nature, are universal qualities. The idea of the Jews as a chosen people was nonsense. Sticking to Mosaic laws after the fall of the second temple in 70 CE was a useless and stubborn form of superstition. He came to these conclusions by reading the Bible not as God's revealed truth, but as a historical text written by men, which should be interpreted with the same intellectual rigor that a sensible person would apply to explorations of nature.

And so, Spinoza concludes that the Jews had "absolutely nothing which they can attribute to themselves beyond all the nations." That they had survived for so long was no surprise, since they had "separated themselves so from all the nations that they have drawn the hatred of all men against themselves, not only by having external customs contrary to the customs of the other nations, but also by the sign of circumcision, which they maintain most scrupulously."[13]

It is hard to think of anything that would cause greater offense to Jews, and particularly to Jews like members of his own family, who had suffered persecution, forced conversion, and were trying so hard in Mokum, the Safe Place, to become practicing Jews again. Spinoza disliked rites and ceremonies in all religions, but his suggestion that Jews had brought the hatred of others upon themselves by refusing to give up their own traditions was especially hurtful. His argument that Jews in Spain who had agreed to convert to Catholicism "received all the native privileges of Spaniards" is also wrong. The "purity of blood" law, imposed in Spain from 1547, made sure that people of Jewish or Muslim ancestry would not receive such privileges, whether they were converted Christians or not. Spinoza's argument for assimilation is naïve, and if it had been made by a gentile, it could easily be construed as a form of antisemitism.

But it was not only Jews who were offended by Spinoza's dismissive views of the Chosen People. Dutch Calvinists were just as likely to be mortified, for in their opposition to Spanish Catholic oppression they identified with the ancient Jews and their struggles for national survival. The return of the Jews to the Holy Land was an essential part of Christian millenarian visions. William the Silent, "Father of the Fatherland," the man who led the Dutch provinces in their sixteenth-century rebellion against the Spanish king, was known as "our Moses," and a session of the States General in 1651 was opened with the words: "Ye children of Israel."[14]

Still, Spinoza's treatment of the Christian faith—though not of manipulative and authoritarian clerics—is much more generous than his criticism of the Jewish religion. The prophets of the Old Testament, in Spinoza's opinion, were men with a superior imagination, whose visions conveyed insights into the workings of God/nature. But, to Spinoza, Christ was greater than them all. In his list of ways to perceive truth, the intuitive understanding of nature was rated more highly than the rationalist, scientific search for truth, and both were of course vastly superior to reliance on gossip, received opinions, and other external influences. Spinoza argued that Christ had achieved a higher degree of perfection than anyone else because "the decisions of God, which lead men to salvation, were revealed immediately—without words or visions." The prophets needed to use their imaginations to get an idea of God. Christ had an intuitive understanding of the truth. He "perceived, truly and adequately what was revealed to him."[15] Even though Spinoza was not without vanity, he would never have admitted this openly, but this interpretation of Christ owes more to Spinoza's self-perception than to the view most Christians had of their savior.

This has prompted one biographer of Spinoza to speculate that he might even have envied Christ's perfect understanding of God. Here is Margaret Gullan-Whur: "I suggest that Spinoza's longing for this state of blessedness was so intense that it tinged his view of Christ with envy, for while he sometimes snapped that Jesus was a prophet who spoke only from imagination, the philosopher also admitted that Christ 'communed with God mind to mind.'"[16]

Perhaps. But why was he so severe in his denunciation of the Jews' insistence on holding on to their customs and laws? And why did he elevate Christ above the Hebrew prophets as a kind of proto philosopher? Was it because Spinoza's nerves were still raw from being expelled by his own people? Or should he be taken at his word when he claims that his knowledge of Christianity, and of the Greek language, were insufficient to study the New Testament as thoroughly as the Hebrew Bible? Was there an element of nostalgia for his Spanish *converso* roots? Or did he suffer from some early form of Stockholm syndrome, and had he taken on some of the antisemitic prejudices of the gentile world in which he lived? Or was he careful not to offend Christian sensibilities, not just of churchmen, but of the more liberal regents as well? He was always acutely aware of social pressures, after all. And he wanted to be convincing to his fellow countrymen.

I don't believe any of these explanations are adequate. Spinoza's comparison between Moses and Christ gives us a better clue. Moses offered his people laws and material rewards. Christ's mission was wholly spiritual. He "was sent, not to preserve the state and to institute laws, but to teach the one universal law."[17] Spinoza's problem with the Jewish idea of being chosen was its particularity, its lack of a universal ideal. His idea of "God's natural law" is meant to apply to everyone—to Jews, Christians, Chinese, Muslims, heathens, indeed everyone without exception. In his words: "It is a law which necessarily follows from human nature."[18] Because the Christian rule to do unto others as you would have them do unto you is supposed to be universal, and the Christian faith, ideally, makes no tribal or national distinctions, it comes closer to Spinoza's idea of a practical civic religion that promotes charity and justice.

Also, Heinrich Heine was not entirely wrong to discern something Christ-like in Spinoza. His saintly insistence on leading a simple, even frugal life, without any romantic attachments, helped to make him a guru-like spiritual figure as well as a philosopher, who didn't promise life after death, but a better life through the cultivation of virtue in the here and now. Those who saw something of the Asian Buddhist in Spinoza would have been nearer the mark if they had compared him to Confucius, the Chinese philosopher who had a similar secular aim to make people behave virtuously in a social order based on harmony and moderation. He, too, applied his philosophy to moral as well as to political behavior.

Although Spinoza thought it would be foolish, as well as perilous, to expose the common man to his philosophical work,

and believed in reason as the way to unlock the secrets of nature, he did not see rationalism as the be all and end all. He even
saw the practical use of the scriptures, especially for the *vulgus.*
The prophets spoke of love and justice. It would be foolish to
reject such messages just because they cannot be mathematically
proven. After all, the wisdom of the prophets "is a great comfort to those whose powers of reason are not strong." This "brings
no slight advantage" to the republic, and can be believed with
absolutely no risk or harm.[19]

One might accuse Spinoza of intellectual arrogance in his
clear division between educated people of reason and the irrational mob. But his notion of promoting a popular faith, based
on scripture, but stripped of all ornament and belief in miracles, was not so very far from the beliefs of his Mennonite and
Collegiant friends who saw Christ as a moral guide rather than
as the literal son of God. There may also be something else at
work, much older than the Mennonites and closer to Spinoza's
own ancestors. Stuart Hampshire explains this well:

> He carried within him, not only suggestions from the theol-
> ogy and biblical criticism of Maimonides and from a great
> line of Jewish scholars and theologians, but also the prophetic
> conception of philosophy as a search for salvation. Although
> salvation by reason substituted in his philosophy for salva-
> tion by revelation and obedience, his moral severity, particu-
> larly if compared with the worldly urbanity of Descartes, is
> often reminiscent of the Old Testament, even in the tone and
> accent of his writing.[20]

I believe this is right. Pierre Bayle reports that friends of
Spinoza said after his death that the philosopher "did not wish
his name to be attached to a sect out of modesty."[21] But Bayle
nonetheless thought that Spinoza had founded a kind of sect to
promote his ideas as a way toward universal salvation.

But there is more to this. Steven Nadler makes a convincing case that Spinoza did not regard himself any longer as a Jew. When writing about the Jews, Spinoza refers to "they" and "them." Not only had he been expelled from the Jewish community, but to be a Jew completely detached from the Jewish faith and Jewish laws would not have made sense to him. Yet he was not a Christian either. He was a loyal citizen of the Dutch Republic, who spoke his national language haltingly with a Portuguese accent. That he saw himself as a thinker who was above tribal, ethnic, or sectarian divisions was not intellectual arrogance; it was a fact. In a modern secular sense, this was the most Jewish thing about him: universalism was his answer to the exclusionary orthodoxy of the rabbis who rejected him, but also a way out of what antisemites liked to call "the Jewish Problem." Almost three centuries after Spinoza's death, Stalin persecuted Jews as "rootless cosmopolitans." Spinoza, in his philosophy, embraced that identity. In his ideal world, distinctions between Jews and gentiles would be seen as so artificial and deluded that they would have to disappear altogether.

8

Radical Enlightenment

ONE ADVANTAGE of living in Voorburg was its proximity to The Hague, which is where the political action was. Amsterdam was the bigger city, but The Hague was, and still is, the seat of government. Spinoza, so Jean Maximilian Lucas tells us, preferred The Hague to Amsterdam anyway, because the air was cleaner. But politics mattered greatly too. The *Theological-Political Treatise* was not just written for the edification of "sensible people," but to influence the regents who governed the republic. According to Colerus, Spinoza made many friends in The Hague in military and other high circles. Lucas even claims that Spinoza was friends with the grand pensionary, Johan de Witt. De Witt is supposed to have asked for instruction in mathematics and consulted Spinoza on other important matters. He is even said to have offered the philosopher an annual stipendium of two hundred guilders.

There is in fact no evidence that the two men ever met in

person. Lucas probably confused De Witt's financial proposition with another, even more generous offer from Simon Joosten
de Vries, Spinoza's most devoted supporter. When the latter, a
man of considerable means, suggested a sum of two thousand
guilders to support his friend, Spinoza politely refused. Mor-
tally ill in 1667, De Vries wanted to leave all his assets to Spinoza. Again, Spinoza said no, thinking the money should go to
De Vries's sister and her husband, who had hosted him at their
country house in Schiedam. De Vries agreed, but on the condition that his brother-in-law pay Spinoza a yearly stipend of five
hundred guilders. Spinoza said that was more than he needed,
and they agreed on three hundred guilders. De Vries was buried in September 1667 next to his mother in one of the finest
Protestant churches in Amsterdam.

De Witt did have a copy of Spinoza's *Treatise* in his library,
and his opponents have claimed that he protected Spinoza's
work after the church authorities called for its ban. Associating
De Witt with Spinoza was a way to taint the grand pensionary
with atheism, which was worse than calling him a crook. There
was even a scurrilous claim that a version of the book found on
De Witt's bookshelf was "produced in hell by the renegade Jew
in collaboration with the Devil, and published in connivance
with Mr. Jan [de Witt] and his accomplices."[1] We don't know
what the grand pensionary actually thought of the *Treatise*. He
would have shared Spinoza's aversion to clerical interference
in secular politics, and he was in favor of freedom of thought—
but only up to a point; he remained a devout Calvinist. De Witt
was also an extremely busy man who was trying to fight a war
with England while keeping the Orangists off his back. He was
not a philosopher or an activist, but a politician who had to
defend his True Freedom rule without turning the Reformed
Church and its monarchist supporters into mortal enemies. That
he would have had an interest in meeting a humble philosopher with a very risky reputation is unlikely. Indeed, when Spi-

noza heard that parts of the *Treatise* alarmed De Witt and asked to see him to explain his ideas in person, De Witt supposedly said that he did "not wish to see such a man cross my threshold."[2]

Spinoza did know people in De Witt's vicinity, however. Christiaan Huygens, the scientific polymath, worked on mathematical problems with De Witt, together with a mathematician named Johannes Hudde, who went on to have an eminent regentesque career that included a stint as mayor of Amsterdam. If Spinoza was ever included in meetings of these three gentlemen, there is no record of it. But Spinoza knew Hudde, with whom he had exchanged views on the best way to polish lenses. And he obviously knew Huygens. Here, too, a shared interest in optics was the basis of their relationship. But a more intimate friendship with Huygens, of the kind Spinoza enjoyed with Meijer or De Vries, was too great a stretch.

The son of Constantijn Huygens, a poet, musician, and secretary of two princes of Orange, Christiaan was a patrician figure, with shoulder-length wigs and French clothes, who spent more time at the Royal Society in London and the court of Louis XIV in Paris than at his elegant family estate in Voorburg. Called Hofwijck, the moated Voorburg house is a classicist gem set in a formal French-style garden, only a short walk away from Spinoza's simple rooms in the village. Both men were fascinated by science, and they exchanged books and ideas, but apart from the obvious social differences, they were too competitive to trust each other. Christiaan, despite his foppish airs, was a practical man with little patience for Spinoza's abstract metaphysical reflections. But he did respect the lens-making skills of the philosopher he called "the Jew of Voorburg," or "the Israelite." Huygens was keen to know how Spinoza managed to craft such fine lenses by hand, even as he himself used more mechanical methods. And he learned from Spinoza that "the small objectives in the microscope represent the objects much more finely than the large ones."[3] Spinoza was clearly intrigued by Huygens's invention of the pendulum clock, as well as his astronomical experiments. And so it happened that they stood together on a clear night in the French garden of Hofwijck, peering through Huygens's telescope at Saturn's ring, which Huygens had been the first to identify. Yet, an edge of suspicion remained. In a letter to his brother, called Constantijn, after their father, Christiaan warns him against giving the Israelite too much information. In letters to Henry Oldenburg, Spinoza was critical of Huygens's views of Descartes. And Oldenburg himself, in a letter to Huygens, makes fun of Spinoza's metaphysical ideas. Exactly why he should do so is unclear; perhaps snobbery was involved, or perhaps Oldenburg wished to ingratiate himself with the Dutch grandee. Partly because Huygens was away so much, he and Spinoza lost touch. But on his deathbed, the patrician scientific genius had lost all faith in a transcendent God and the immortality of the soul. His work on the planets and the life-forms detected through his microscope left him feeling that God and nature were the same thing. As a recent biographer of Huygens observed, this was "an idea crystallized by the Dutch 'Golden Age.' Certainly, it was one that found concise philosophical expression in the words of Huygens's sometime neighbor, supplier and co-worker Baruch Spinoza, whose *Ethics* drew God and Nature into an identity."[4]

Spinoza's *Treatise* was as much a product of the Golden Age as Rembrandt's *Nightwatch* or Vermeer's *View of Delft*. For a work of genius to emerge, the right time and place is needed for fellow artists and thinkers to inspire one another, as well as a receptive audience. Spinoza expressed his ideas on religion and politics with greater brilliance than his peers, but his book did not appear out of thin air. The *Treatise* was the masterpiece of what Jonathan Israel has called the Radical Enlightenment, the Dutch forerunner to the eighteenth-century philosophes, and an uncompromising alternative to the more flexible nature of the English and Scottish Enlightenment.[5] But others were working on similar ideas in Holland and publishing bold books, which were sometimes banned, sometimes *gedoogd*, and often circulated in private. A few even became bestsellers. Writing in Dutch was more dangerous than writing in Latin, since the church authorities feared that wider access would corrupt the common man. And the most daring texts were published anonymously or with fake imprints, almost invariably by the estimable Jan Rieuwertsz. Most of the authors were Spinoza's close friends from Amsterdam and Leiden, even if he didn't often acknowledge their influence on his own work. He was not a guru for nothing.

Spinoza's former Latin teacher, Franciscus van den Enden, published *Free Political Institutions* (Vrye politieke stellingen) in 1665. A fierce opponent of monarchism, he advocated social equality, freedom of speech, and popular sovereignty. Van den Enden was influenced by Machiavelli, but even more by two other Dutchmen of the Radical Enlightenment, Pieter and Johan de la Court. The brothers were confirmed republicans who denied that any form of monarchical or aristocratic rule could ever be based on popular consent. They agreed with Hobbes, whose great influence hovers over all the freethinkers of his time, including Spinoza, that a stable polity was necessary to protect people from the state of nature. But they didn't think that a monarch was best placed to secure a stable polity. And unlike Hobbes, they did not believe that nature was necessarily brutal. Natural rights could be maintained in a civilized society. They also thought that "the few must conform to the wishes of the many. This natural equity is the basis of all democracy, or popular sovereignty."[6] But if popular sovereignty was going to work, people needed to be enlightened and well informed. This was Van den Enden's main argument for popular education. It was time to wrest knowledge from the academic, professional, and ecclesiastical elites who protected their authority behind a misty veil of Latin and other foreign jargon. Van den Enden also regarded himself as a man of action, who offered De Witt help in devising secret weapons against the English (De Witt showed no interest). Later, as mentioned before, he was hanged for conspiring against the French king.

Two close friends of Spinoza, Adriaan Koerbagh and Dr. Lodewijk Meijer, put Van den Enden's words into practice. Meijer's *Dutch Lexicon* (Nederlandsche woordenschat) was published in 1669. The goal was to educate the public by translating Latin and other foreign technical and scientific terms into plain Dutch. If doctors, lawyers, and theologians were bothered by Meijer's lexicon, the Reformed clerics were much more upset by his *Philosophy as the Interpreter of Scripture* (see Chapter Five), in which Meijer argued that only a philosophical—that is, a scientific—interpretation of the Bible would yield any truths. Since rational thinking could arrive at those truths just as well, the implication was that theology was no longer required. This book, written in Latin and later translated by Meijer into Dutch, did not bear his name, and was printed as an underground publication by Rieuwertsz. Meijer was much reviled, of course, but also widely discussed. As he had predicted: "The discomfort and harm, which hang above my head, is the hatred of the theologians."[7] But his writing did not land him in prison, unlike what happened to his friend Koerbagh, who also tried to enlighten the common man in his own language, but in a far more dangerous and provocative manner.

Adriaan and his younger brother, Johannes, were born to a middle-class family in Amsterdam. Their father, a ceramicist, died young, and the boys were raised in regent circles. A well-known lawyer and cousin of Jan de Witt was appointed as their guardian. Adriaan studied law and medicine at several universities, including Leiden, where he and his brother had frequent meetings with Spinoza, probably in the late 1650s. Johannes, a church minister, drew the attention of Reformed authorities by attending Collegiant meetings in Amsterdam, where, as a proper Calvinist cleric, he had no business to be. Adriaan invited their disapproval for "whoring" and "licentiousness"—he had had a child out of wedlock. Johannes was the first to be grilled on his views by the orthodox churchmen. His answers were unsatisfactory, and his duties as a pastor were suspended.

But it was Adriaan's books that got the brothers into more serious trouble. His first published works were follow-ups on Meijer's lexicon. In 1666 he wrote a lexicon of his own, explaining Latin legal terms in Dutch. More inflammatory was his next book, in 1668, with the remarkable title *A Flower Garden of All Kinds of Loveliness, Planted without Sorrow* (Een bloemhof van allerley lieflijkheyd sonder verdriet). Not content to simply translate religious and technical words from Latin, Greek, French, or Hebrew into Dutch, he supplied commentaries that were very disobliging to the clergy, not only of the Jewish and Catholic persuasion, but Calvinists too. The word *Bible*, he said, just meant "book" in Greek, and it was no different from an ordinary book of fairy tales. Angels, another Greek word, were not supernatural beings, but messengers, no more holy than postmen. Prophets predict things in the future that "seldom come true," and whatever they say is "always ambiguous or obscure." The Reformed Church was not the same as popery, to be sure, but still "far removed from a true religion, based on wisdom, truth, and reason."[8]

Koerbagh's *Flower Garden* was an instant success when it came out in 1668. The Reformed Church council immediately tried to get the city authorities to ban the book. The authorities said this was a most serious affair and promised to investigate the matter, without in fact taking any action, which was their usual ploy to dodge such religious squabbles. Still, Adriaan thought it wiser to keep his head down in a provincial town, where he was less likely to be bothered. Johannes was interrogated once again, and although he denied having had anything to do with his brother's book, he was detained "in the hope that he might escape from the embrace of Satan."[9]

Meanwhile, Adriaan attempted to get an even more seditious book published, which was *A Light Shining in Dark Places, To Illuminate the Main Questions of Theology and Religion*. Apart from a change in terminology here and there, the content of this book is very close to Spinoza's ideas: miracles are absurd; God is the unique, eternal, self-perpetuating substance, and "the origin of reason"; reason must be followed "in all things, spiritual, political, and scientific," and "the government entrusted with authority by the people will instill the laws to make the people peaceful and the country prosperous."[10] Koerbagh's book still reads a little like a religious text, but with "reason" substituted for "faith." He would have approved of the shrine to the Goddess of Reason erected in the Notre Dame cathedral by French revolutionaries a century later. His loathing of the clergy almost surpasses that of Voltaire and other philosophes: "What cruel persecutions and cursed fratricides [the clerics] are responsible for! Oh, the horror, the horror of horrors!"[11]

Koerbagh did not put his own name to this remarkable tract. It was supposedly written by Vreederijk Waarmond (Peaceful Truemouth), a "researcher in truth." Alas, before it was even half finished, the printer in Utrecht got cold feet, refused to continue printing the book, and handed the manuscript over to the sheriff's office. From there it was passed into the hands of the Amsterdam sheriff. Once again, poor Johannes was questioned rather severely as the suspected author. When he denied it, the magistrates offered a reward of one thousand guilders to anyone who could deliver Adriaan from his hiding place. A young man, who claimed he knew where to find him, asked for three times that amount, but betrayed Adriaan anyway when the authorities stuck to their original offer.

Adriaan was taken to Amsterdam, where he was tortured in

a cell under the imposing town hall, which is now the royal palace on Dam Square. This was also the place where people received their death sentences amid skulls and heads of Medusa beautifully carved in marble. One of the magistrates who witnessed Koerbagh's torments was Johannes Hudde, the mathematician who exchanged notes with Spinoza on the grinding of lenses. Hudde may have helped to soften Koerbagh's sentence. After admitting that he was indeed the author of the books, Koerbagh was asked whether Van den Enden or Spinoza had influenced him in any way. Koerbagh said that he had spoken to both men, but that they knew nothing of his writings. This may not have been entirely true. Koerbagh was clearly not just a learned man, but also courageous and loyal to his friends. The prosecutor demanded that the wretched blasphemer be hanged outside the town hall. But first he would have to spend thirty years in prison, and that would happen only after his thumb was cut from his right hand and a hot spike driven through his tongue. The magistrates, possibly persuaded by Hudde, decided on a less draconian sentence: ten years in prison, ten years of banishment from Amsterdam, and a four thousand guilder fine. Koerbagh's books were burned in public. A poem was later circulated about the affair, which went:

> Koerbagh, how lucky you were
> to be arrested because of a dictionary
> in the great city on the Amstel.
> If you had been behind bars in Italy or Spain
> your punishment would have been worse than the gallows.[12]

Quite possibly. But brutally hard labor in a notoriously harsh prison—the old gate of which, adorned with sculptures of naked prisoners in chains, still survives as the façade of a fashionable shopping mall—were too much for the gentle idealist. He died an ill and broken man less than a year later. When his funeral bier was borne through the center of Amsterdam by black-suited men, a crowd of onlookers spotted a pitch-black hen that refused to leave its perch on the coffin, despite stones being thrown. There was no doubt in the minds of the mob that Satan himself was accompanying the wicked heretic to his grave.

We can only guess at Spinoza's feelings about the shocking fate of his friend. Whatever correspondence there had been between the two men would have been destroyed for obvious reasons. There are no references to Koerbagh in the letters that remained. But that a good friend had been persecuted to death for writing a book that was so close to Spinoza's own ideas must have been more than disconcerting. It would explain why the *Treatise* Spinoza was working on was more urgent and acerbic in tone than anything else he ever wrote. It was also, no doubt, why Spinoza was careful only to publish his ideas anonymously and in Latin.

The year before Koerbagh's arrest, True Freedom had a moment of great triumph, while also starting to buckle under pressure from the clergy and the Orangists. These fissures would end in mob violence and the horrible deaths of Johan de Witt and his devoted brother, Cornelis. The triumph came after the Dutch navy boldly sailed up the Thames in June 1667, with Cornelis de Witt on deck of the admiral's flagship, and broke the chain across the river, leaving the Royal Navy at its mercy. Samuel Pepys recorded what happened in his diary on June 12: "Home, where all our hearts do now ache; for the news is true, that the Dutch have broke the chain and burned our ships, including the Royal Charles; other particulars I know not, but most sad, to be sure. And, the truth is, I do fear so much that the whole kingdom is undone."[13]

Peace was signed on August 5, 1667, after a ruinously expensive war. There was dancing in the streets of The Hague, where the crowds got drunk on cheap beer, while the regents celebrated in their townhouses with fine French wines and game marinated in rich French sauces. Even so, the war had weakened De Witt's government enough to force the grand pensionary to agree to a new edict that allowed Prince William of Orange to become a member of the State Council and eventually captain-general of the Dutch armed forces. The Orange faction soon became a powerful clique undermining the authority of the De Witts wherever it could, while hoping to reinstall the prince as stadtholder. The cruel sentencing of Koerbagh was a sign that the *gedoog* policy of the regents was no longer strong enough to resist the church that backed the House of Orange.

Spinoza declared his political sentiments in the prologue to the *Treatise:*

> Since, then, we happen to have that rare good fortune—that we live in a Republic in which everyone is granted complete freedom of judgment, and is permitted to worship God according to his mentality, and in which nothing is thought to be dearer or sweeter than freedom, I believed I would be doing something neither unwelcome, nor useless, if I showed not only that this freedom can be granted without harm to piety and the peace of the Republic, but also that it cannot be abolished unless piety and the peace of the Republic are abolished with it.[14]

Spinoza knew perfectly well that freedom, even during the Golden Age of Rembrandt and the De Witts, was not unlimited. Some scholars conclude from this that he was either being sarcastic in his praise or flattering the class of people he wanted to persuade. There may, however, be a different way to read this. Even though the Dutch Republic under True Freedom came well short of Spinoza's democratic ideal, he felt he had to defend it. Popular sovereignty of the kind the de la Court brothers, Van den Enden, Koerbagh, or indeed Spinoza himself advocated was not yet on offer. Even the greatest proponents of a Radical Enlightenment had not worked out how exactly a democracy would work. Spinoza certainly hadn't. But he was clear in his own mind what freedom meant to him, and who were its main enemies.

The most important freedom for Spinoza was the freedom to use reason, to investigate nature, as well as human affairs (which were after all part of nature) rationally—in a word, to philosophize. The free man is one who has learned to understand nature, his own and the nature of all things around him. This cannot be achieved in "the state of nature." Like Hobbes, Spinoza believed that people are naturally selfish and thus inclined to satisfy their own desires and do anything for self-preservation. Spinoza's Latin term for this was *conatus*. To prevent a struggle of all against all, and to keep people safe from violence, political organization was necessary, as a matter of rational self-interest. Laws were essential to distinguish between right and wrong, not as moral strictures revealed by God, but as man-made rules to stop us from killing each other. Where Spinoza and Hobbes differed was in their thoughts on what kind of organization this required.

Hobbes took a pessimistic view of human nature and believed that natural appetites could only be curbed by investing a single sovereign, preferably a monarch, with absolute power. Individuals would have to give up all their natural rights for the sake of their security. Spinoza did not go nearly that far. To him, the freedom to think and express one's thoughts was sacrosanct. He was convinced that any ruler's attempt to stifle it would inevitably end in failure, for people would surely rebel. A government should have the power to make laws and force people to obey them, but such power was only legitimate, and effective, so long as it safeguarded the interests of the governed.

To hand over power to a monarch, Spinoza argued, is senseless anyway, since kings look out for their own interests and become tyrants who rule by terror from fear of being overthrown.

Once a tyranny by monarchs is established, it is very difficult to get rid of it, even by assassinating a tyrant, for he will quickly be replaced by another, so long as the tyrannical system stays intact. And the new tyrant will behave exactly as his predecessor: "That's how it happens that the people can often change the tyrant, but can never destroy him, or change a monarchic state into another, of a different form."[15]

Aristocratic rule is no better, for it will perpetuate the power of a small, closed circle, based on family bloodlines, that won't take much notice of the common good. Democracy, he argued, was best suited to preserving human freedom, since sovereignty belonged to everyone, and not just to a happy few, who would have to convince the masses that they had a special, even divine, right to rule over them. But here Spinoza seems to have run into a paradox. For he agreed with Hobbes that everyone needed to obey the sovereign power, voluntarily or out of fear of punishment. In other words, for the people to exercise their sovereign power, they had to give up their individual powers. But this was a price worth paying, because democracy was the most likely system to uphold reason and the common good. An assembly of reasonable men, elected by reasonable people (though not by women and servants), will act reasonably. It is rare in an equitable system for the highest authorities to give totally unreasonable orders. After all, "To look out for their own interests and retain their sovereignty, it is incumbent on them most of all to consult the common good, and to direct everything according to the dictate of reason."[16]

Spinoza's idea of democracy, outlined in the *Treatise*, is as abstract as a mathematical theorem. He would work these ideas out much more concretely in his *Political Treatise* (Tractatus politicus) at the end of his life. At this stage, he also left out historical contingency. And yet, to illustrate his points, he came up with two examples, neither of them perfect, but they were the best he could do, and closest to him personally—one from the distant past and one exactly contemporary: the Hebrew state under Moses, and the seventeenth-century Dutch Republic.

When the ancient Hebrews elected Moses to decree God's laws, and power was divided among the twelve tribes of Israel (an arrangement Spinoza compared to the United Provinces of the Netherlands), the Hebrew state was both a theocracy, since God ruled, and something comparable to a democracy. All God's subjects had agreed to obey one central authority, which was God, and had the same right to consult God, interpret his laws, and govern the state. High priests were teachers but had no worldly powers. They couldn't impose their views or excommunicate citizens. There was no aristocracy either. And the state was defended against its enemies by a citizen army of equals.

Things only started going wrong after the death of Moses, when tyrants ruled the land and priests grabbed political powers, which caused religion to degenerate into poisonous superstitions that split society into warring sects. Spinoza's potted history of the ancient Hebrews may not be historically accurate, but his intention is clear. He is not suggesting that the state under Moses could be imitated, or even that such a thing would be desirable. Instead, he uses the rise and fall of the Hebrew state as a metaphor for Dutch politics. Near the end of the *Treatise*, he writes about the bloody consequences of religious sectarianism and priestly interference in the making of laws. Nothing is stupider than to legislate against the dissident opinions of decent men: "What greater evil can be imagined for the Republic than that honest men should be exiled as wicked because they hold different opinions and don't know how to pretend to be what they're not? Or that the scaffold, the scourge of the evil, should become the noblest stage for displaying the utmost endurance and the model of virtue, to the conspicuous shame of the majesty?"[17]

Spinoza might have had Koerbagh in mind, but he was also

alluding to the execution in 1619 of Johan van Oldenbarneveldt, the liberal leader of the Dutch Republic, and the arrest of his ally, Hugo Grotius, after an insurrection whipped up by orthodox Calvinists, and supported by Maurits, the prince of Orange. That is what happens, Spinoza warned, when priests and aristocrats get their hands on political power.

Here and there in the *Treatise*, Spinoza makes a direct comment on contemporary Dutch politics, which shows his deep attachment to the republic of True Freedom. He writes: "As for the States of Holland, so far as we know they never had Kings, but only counts, to whom the right to rule was never transferred. . . . From this it follows that the states always had the right of supreme majesty, a right the last count tried to usurp."[18] There is some disagreement about which usurper he was referring to. The most likely candidate is the stadtholder William II, prince of Orange, and count of Orange-Nassau, who led the failed military coup in 1650.

Some writers on Spinoza have suggested that he was a protofascist, or at least a totalitarian thinker, because he believed that the state should have complete control over religious affairs and institutions. He did indeed think that religious worship and practices should serve the interests of the state. They should be solely determined by the highest (state) authorities. One might call this kind of state power over spiritual affairs totalitarian, but that would be anachronistic. Spinoza could not have foreseen twentieth-century dictatorships that attempted to control people's minds by turning political dogmas into quasi-religious justifications for total power. The main threat to intellectual freedom in his time was the imposition of religious doctrine by church authorities. He didn't, in any case, advocate that individual piety or thinking should be dictated by the state. People should be free to believe or think what they wanted. But their actions should not be allowed to actively undermine state authority. The state should only be concerned with the outward forms of religious worship, not of piety itself or the inner worship of God. After all, Spinoza said, "The worship of God and obedience to him consists only in Justice and Loving-kindness, or in love toward one's neighbor."[19] Whether God's commandment of justice and love came from the true understanding of nature or from sacred revelation was a matter of indifference to him, so long as people behaved in a peaceful and orderly manner. Since most people were not philosophers, equipped to understand nature, a kind of civic religion was required to ensure the obedience of citizens to a reasonable government that worked for the benefit of all.

With the benefit of hindsight, we can dismiss Spinoza's idea of a civic religion—an official creed promoting a sense of civility, obedience to lawful authority, and justice—as naïve or undemocratic, but it was close to what the French aristocrat Alexis de Tocqueville thought about American democracy two centuries later. Although Tocqueville was in some ways still a figure of the ancien régime, he was a sympathetic observer of democracy. American democracy worked, he argued, because the rule of law and the will of the majority were underpinned by a strong collective belief in Christian morality. But Tocqueville didn't see a civic religion as a means to impose obedience to the state. In his not unambivalent view, social cohesion in America came from conformity to the religious mores of the Protestant majority. Unlike Thomas Jefferson, however, Spinoza did insist on state control of religious practices. This was certainly radical for his time. Was it also illiberal? The answer rather depends on what one thinks Spinoza meant by individual freedom. This is complicated by his conviction that everything, including human behavior, is determined by nature.

9

—◆◄◆►◆—

Mob Rage

SPINOZA WAS IN THE FINISHING STAGES of his *Theological-Political Treatise* in the fall of 1669, when he moved from the relative seclusion of Voorburg to the hurly-burly of The Hague. The first year there he lived in the house of a lawyer's widow named Van der Werve, in the same second-floor rooms where his biographer Johannes Colerus would settle twenty years later. But the rent was steep, so Spinoza moved to a house around the corner, on the Paviljoensgracht, owned by the master painter Hendrick van der Spyck. Spinoza was, by all accounts, an easygoing, accommodating lodger who would often go days without emerging from his room. He had an ivory chess set, a game that was considered rather upper class at the time (most people preferred cards), and he amused himself by watching spiders fight in a little box; this made him laugh. A similar entertainment was offered by sticking live flies onto a spider's web to see what would happen. But when he was in the mood for company,

Spinoza would climb down the stairs to spend time with Van der Spyck, his wife, Ida, and their three children. He would pull out his clay pipe and chat happily about the trivial affairs of daily life.

Spinoza's frail health, increasingly weakened by tuberculosis, was one reason for his move to The Hague. Even the relatively short trips on foot or by boat from Voorburg were becoming too exhausting. Lucas also mentions that Spinoza was "not insensible to the genuine affection of people of quality." Among them, it is said, were "young girls of good family who took pride in being more intelligent than most members of their sex."[1]

Whether or not this was true—the story of the young girls is pure hearsay—The Hague had a special atmosphere. As the center of government and diplomacy, and the residence of the princes of Orange, the town put on aristocratic airs, unlike the merchant city of Amsterdam, where even the patrician regents were mostly in business. William Temple, the English ambassador who arranged the marriage between Prince William of Orange and Princess Mary of England, reported that people of The Hague tried "to imitate the French, in their mien, their clothes, their way of talk, of eating, of gallantry, of debauchery."[2] Despite several wars with France and a military occupation in the early nineteenth century under Napoleon's brother, this habit of mimicking the style of a foreign elite persisted. When I grew up in The Hague, some snobbish people still larded their Dutch with French expressions, but the *style anglais*, or what Italians call *gentlemanismo*, had largely become the norm among the haute bourgeoisie after World War Two.

Spinoza was not a snob in any superficial sense. He dressed in a sober fashion, ate very simply, and never attended dinner parties, let alone balls or anything of that sort. But he did, as we have already seen, make a clear distinction between what he called "sensible people," people endowed with reason, who could understand the point of philosophy, and the common people, led by their passions. Some of his sensible friends in Amsterdam, such as Lodewijk Meijer and Johannes Bouwmeester, met regularly to discuss the arts and the theater, as well as Spinozist ideas in a society called Nothing Is Impossible for Those Who Have the Will (Nil Volentibus Arduum). In The Hague, the style was quite Frenchified. Political freethinkers looked to the intellectual libertines of Paris.

When the *Treatise* was published in 1670, by Jan Rieuwertsz, it didn't bear Spinoza's name. On the title page it says, quite misleadingly, that the book was published in Hamburg. When Spinoza was told of plans to publish a Dutch translation of the *Treatise*, he wrote a letter to his Amsterdam friend Jarig Jellesz, expressing his dismay: "I beg you, very earnestly, to please find out about this, to prevent the printing, if that's possible. This is not only my request, but also that of many of my good friends, who would not like to see this book prohibited. If it's published in Dutch, that will doubtless happen. I don't doubt that you will do me and the cause this service."[3]

No doubt caution was one reason for Spinoza's alarm. What happened to Adriaan Koerbagh was still fresh in his memory. Even in the Latin edition, the *Treatise* came in for some heavy criticism and was later proscribed; it certainly would not have been tolerated in Dutch. But Spinoza's decision was not only driven by prudence: he hated the idea of being hampered by fear; that was the mark of an unfree man. There was also a political reason for his refusal of a translation. Unlike Koerbagh, Van den Enden, or Meijer, Spinoza was not a populist who believed that all people could be so easily enlightened once specialized knowledge was wrested from the elites. If royal tyrants and bigoted clerics were a threat to freethinking and speech, so were crowds whipped up into a frenzy by malevolent leaders. Schisms and civil strife did not come from the pursuit of truth, but from leaders who condemned certain books and "incite the unruly mob" against the men who wrote them.

During his life, and to this day, Spinoza has been seen as a radical figure, wicked and dangerous to some, a democratic hero to others. But he was no revolutionary, unlike his Latin teacher. Acts of violence, provoked by passions, are contrary to reason. He made a distinction between dissidents and rebels. It is perfectly legitimate for a citizen to argue that unreasonable laws should be changed, but he must obey the law while it is still in force. Yet when the critic turns the people against the legislators in hate and tries to overturn the law with violence, he is a rioter. Since Spinoza believed that most people are more liable to be ruled by their passions than by reason, it was essential to learn how to moderate those passions lest they disturb the peace and make freethinking impossible. In this sense, Spinoza was hardly a proto-Jacobin, unlike some of his friends in Amsterdam, whose revolutionary egalitarianism was more in line with the eighteenth-century rebels who toppled the French king in the name of the people's will.

That Spinoza was a rationalist does not mean that he thought human desires could ever be completely tamed, or even that this would be a good thing. Joy and pleasure are to be encouraged. They are essential aspects of *conatus*, the natural life force, the instinctual urge to continue living. In Spinoza's *Ethics*, the writing of which he took up once more when the *Treatise* was done, he claims that only "a grim and sad superstition resists joy." The more we feel joy, the closer we are to our true nature, and thus to God. The wise man should relish pleasure ("though not to excess, for then it ceases to be a pleasure"). He should "restore himself in moderation with pleasant food and drink, with scents, with the beauty of green plants, with decoration, music, sports, the theater, and other things of this kind, which anyone can use without injury to another."[4] Human beings are as much a part of nature as a horse or an ape. To have desires is natural, but to be slaves to our desires makes us unfree. In *Ethics*,

Spinoza analyzes the variety of human desires, and the ways we can master them, with the logical rigor of a geometric problem.

The idea of *conatus*, and the assumption that human beings are wired to follow their desires, raises some tricky questions. What about people who seek to destroy themselves—not an uncommon affliction, after all? Spinoza deals with suicide rather summarily. The wish to kill oneself goes against natural laws, and those who give in to such a compulsion are "weak-minded and completely conquered by external causes contrary to their nature."[5] The more a person is affected by circumstances beyond his control, the less free he is. The more a person's actions arise from her own nature, the freer she will be.

If desires are natural, why should we moderate them? That oversaturation diminishes pleasure is one reason. But Spinoza also returns to his argument for a stable democratic order. The lives of most people are not ruled by reason. It is more common for people to envy others and stand in each other's way. And yet, we are social animals, and there are more advantages than disadvantages to living in a community. Desire is good, Spinoza argues, especially if it comes from joy, and not sadness, because desire gives us the zest for life; it helps us to survive. Since reason, he continues, demands nothing that is contrary to nature, a reasonable person will desire what is good for him or herself. Ideally, this desire, this reasonable life force will match the desires of others, and as a result will make us all stronger. In a clear nod toward Christian morality, Spinoza also proposes that to live a life of reason, we must "repay the other's Hate with Love, i.e. with Nobility."[6]

Since Spinoza was also convinced that everything, including our natural desires and our thoughts, is determined by nature, and affected by external circumstances, he needed to explain how the passions, as well as those outside influences, could be tempered by the intellect. In his *Ethics*, Spinoza ridicules Descartes's idea of a God-given free will. There is no such thing. For Descartes the physical world, which can be measured, and the mental world of thought belonged to two distinct, self-contained systems. Spinoza, however, did not make that distinction. Both mind and body (meaning all physical emanations of nature) arrived from the same indivisible substance that is God, or nature. The body cannot exist without a corresponding mind, and a mind cannot exist without a corresponding body. Our minds cannot tell the body what to do, or the other way around. But we can still think and act, and so long as we are guided by reason, we will "want, *or* follow, only the greater good and the lesser evil."[7] These acts of thinking, in Spinoza's view, are how we exercise our will. The more we are guided by reason, and the less we are at the mercy of our passions and situations beyond our control, the better we understand our true nature, the closer we are to God, the easier it will be to use good judgment, and the happier and freer we will be.

Spinoza ends his *Ethics* on a rather wry note. He has to admit that his prescription for the rational, free, good life is extremely hard to achieve. Indeed, he wonders "if salvation were at hand, and could be found without great effort, how could nearly everyone neglect it? But all things excellent are as difficult as they are rare."[8]

This still leaves the question of what to do with the unreasoning masses, who are easily manipulated by malevolent leaders and malicious priests. On the vices of the average *homme moyen sensuel*, of people who overindulge their desires, and so on, he is broad-minded. There is no point in cracking down on those passions by law unless they do active harm to the state. He already pointed out in the *Treatise* how a civic religion based on scripture and focused on justice and charity should ensure popular obedience to the essential rules and laws of a democratic state.

Spinoza applied this principle in his own relations with

people outside his philosophical circles, such as the family he was living with in The Hague. Colerus relates that he urged the children to obey their elders and go to church. When their mother asked Spinoza whether he thought her faith would save her, he replied there was nothing wrong with her faith, and she would be saved so long as she lived a virtuous life. He even had words of praise for their Lutheran pastor and encouraged the family to attend the services of this excellent man. At the same time, Spinoza attacked religious superstitions that worked on people's hopes and fears—fear of divine punishment in the afterlife, and hope of living in heaven after the irksome restrictions of earthly existence have been left behind.

Nonetheless, and this might seem like a contradiction, even Spinoza saw some use in fearfulness to correct the violent impulses of the mob. One of the emotions examined in the *Ethics* is repentance, which, he argues, is not a virtue, since it doesn't come from reason. Repentance isn't reasonable, because our views on what is good or bad are a matter of upbringing and prejudice and not laws of nature. What some people regard as good, others see as bad. We regret something we did because we were overwhelmed by a base desire, and then feel sad about it afterward. However, since most people don't live their lives according to the laws of reason, "Humility and Repentance, and in addition, Hope and Fear, bring more advantage than disadvantage." After all, if weak-minded people felt no fear or shame, they would easily get out of hand. The fearless mob, he writes, is a terrifying thing, which is why the prophets, who sought the welfare of all people, and not just individuals, put such store on humility, repentance, and obedience. To solve the contradiction in what he has just proposed, Spinoza ends his argument by saying that humble, contrite, and obedient people "can be guided far more easily than others, so that in the end they may live from the guidance of reason, i.e., may be free and enjoy the life of the blessed."[9]

* * *

Everything Spinoza most feared came to pass in 1672, the Catastrophic Year (*Rampjaar*), when True Freedom finally came crashing down. Things had not gone well in the years leading up to the disaster. The Dutch Republic was a trading nation, governed by regents with business and not military affairs on their minds. Defenses, especially on land, had been neglected. No one wanted to pay for a strong army. Fortresses on the borders with the German states and the Southern Netherlands were in bad shape. Louis XIV of France was gearing up to take advantage of the weakness of a small Protestant country, and England's King Charles was always looking for ways to cut the Dutch down to size at sea and in the colonies. Johan and Cornelis de Witt tried their best to keep their nation safe through diplomacy. Spain, the old archenemy, was approached as a potential ally against the French, without much success. Sweden and Denmark, who might have been obvious Protestant allies, were paid by the French to stay out of conflicts with the Dutch Republic. And even as the Royal Navy was stalking Dutch ships, and French troops moved farther and farther north, the bishop of Münster and the archbishop of Cologne threatened to invade from the east.

The Dutch Republic of merchants was under siege from kings and clerics who believed they had the divine right to rule. Instead of this pulling the Dutch provinces together, a panicky atmosphere inflamed divisions between Orangists and regents, rural folk and city folk, church and state. Resentment against the regents and the urban elites, accused of being Francophile, soft, and corrupt, began to boil over. More and more people clamored for Prince William of Orange, who was barely in his twenties, to save them. De Witt had to agree, very much against his will, to appoint Prince William as captain-general of the army and admiral of the navy. Celebrations in The Hague turned riotous, when drunken militiamen and gangs of hooligans roamed through the streets shooting in the air and smashing the windows of regents' houses, while singing "Long Live the Prince of Orange!"

In April, England became the first country to attack the Dutch at sea. The French navy joined the English, but the Dutch still had some formidable battleships, and a joint Anglo-French naval force was fought to a standstill off the Suffolk coast with Cornelis de Witt, suffering from gout, watching the proceedings from his armchair on deck of the Dutch flagship. But the Dutch army, a ragtag bunch of ill-trained soldiers recruited at the last minute, could not prevent vastly superior French troops from invading the republic. Louis XIV's army, led by the prince of Condé, behaved like *conquistadores,* burning villages to the ground, massacring civilians, looting homes and livestock, and raping wives and daughters in front of their husbands and fathers. Only breaking the dikes and flooding large areas, much to the chagrin of local farmers, who tried to sabotage this defensive measure, prevented the French from occupying The Hague and Amsterdam.

Popular blame for the national calamity fell squarely on the De Witt brothers and their patrician government, especially when people saw wealthy regents put their possessions in storage and take to the boats bound for safer regions, even as refugees from French occupation came swarming into the cities. The streets of The Hague became increasingly lawless as mobs cried for installing Prince William as the new stadtholder and death to the "traitors" who had brought ruin on the Netherlands. Pamphlets were distributed denouncing the De Witts as the sons of Satan. It was no longer safe for Johan de Witt to walk the short distance from his home to his office. One night he was accosted by men who slashed his face and chest with swords. Darkness protected him from worse. When one of the would-be assassins was caught and sentenced to death, he was hailed as a martyr from the Dutch Reformed pulpits. Preachers called for a purge of sinners and the destruction of "poisonous weeds" in the garden of Holland. "Up with Orange, down with De Witts!," cried the rabble, out for the blood of the hated upper classes.

While Johan de Witt was recuperating from his wounds, men barged into the house of Cornelis to kill him in his bed. Only the timely intervention of one of his servants prevented the murder. More violence was in the air. A popular verse about Johan went: "De Witt revived from his wounds? / What terrible news / the country would be saved, if he were dead / But he is alive."[10] The authority of his government was now so weak that Prince William was installed as stadtholder, and Johan de Witt resigned as grand pensionary. True Freedom was over; the House of Orange, supported by the Reformed clergy, was back.

Cornelis got himself involved in a murky affair that was never entirely cleared up. He was visited in his home by a barber with an unsavory reputation, who supposedly offered to kill the stadtholder for the right price. There is no evidence that Cornelis agreed to this proposal, but when the story came out, he lied and said that he had never even met the man. This was reason enough for the Orangists to have him arrested as a traitor. He was flung in jail in The Hague, where he was tortured for three and a half hours while crowds milled outside the prison gate. Cornelis was hung upside down, his shoulders were dislocated, his ankles broken, his forehead squeezed in a vise, and he was soundly whipped. But he confessed to nothing. Still, a court sentenced him to banishment from Holland for life.

A sign appeared beside the door of the New Church, where Spinoza would later be buried. It read: "Beelzebub writes from hell that Kees [short for Cornelis] de Witt is coming / he is expected there soon / but not before his head comes off."[11] Preachers were no less vicious in their sermons, which called for the devil to be driven out to restore God-fearing virtue to the land.

The usual rabble of armed militias and violent townsmen threatened to drag Cornelis out of his cell when a rumor started that he was about to flee. In fact, he was in his bed reading a play by Molière, while Johan was reading the Bible by his side. The crowd, incited by a silversmith named Verhoeff, was banging on the prison gate, screaming, "Up with Orange, down with De Witt!" Possibly ordered to do so by officers on the prince's side, official armed forces withdrew from the scene, leaving the center of The Hague in the hands of the mob. Prince William refused to go in person to calm the crowd down.

Finally, the prison doors were forced open, and the brothers were dragged out to face a pack of screaming people pointing rifles, swords, knives, and halberds at them. Johan was shot in the back, and Cornelis was beaten to death by a butcher and a fishmonger. This was only the beginning. The two corpses were suspended upside down from the gallows. Fingers were hacked off, tongues ripped out, and the innards were exposed by butchers. Verhoeff, the silversmith, carried the brothers' hearts in triumph through the streets. One man tried to bite off Cornelis's testicles. Women danced in a frenzy after wrapping themselves in the slippery intestines. Nipples, fingers, ears, and noses were grabbed as souvenirs. More and more people came to gawk at the grisly scenes.

Spinoza, whose rooms were only a short walk away from the lynch party, was beside himself when he heard what was happening. Lucas relates that Spinoza wept at the idea of "his fellow-citizens tearing the man who was a father to them all to pieces. Even though he knew better than anyone what men are capable of, he still shuddered at this terrible and cruel spectacle."[12] Spinoza later told people that his landlord, Hendrick van der Spyck, had to physically restrain him from going out that night to place a placard at the site of the crimes that read "*ultimi barbarorum*," meaning "the lowest of barbarians." A good thing too, for even though most common people, led by their passions, wouldn't have been able to read those words in Latin, enough would, and Spinoza would not have come back alive.

This was clearly not the right time to publish his *Ethics*. The reception of the *Treatise* had been bad enough. Despite his name not appearing on the cover of his book, it soon leaked out that Spinoza was the author. Already in 1670, Samuel Maresius, a French Protestant professor in Groningen who had studied under Franciscus Gomarus, the scourge of the Arminians, denounced the "atrocious book" written by Spinoza, "ex-Jew, blasphemer and former atheist."[13] Church bodies in many Dutch cities demanded that the book be banned, along with Hobbes's *Leviathan*. Even Cartesians, frightened that they might be associated with Spinoza, piled on with attacks of their own. While Johan de Witt was still in power, the government dragged its feet on a ban, even as the regents tut-tutted to appease the outraged clergy. De Witt himself was supposed to have worried that Spinoza's writings would encourage the common people to behave in licentious ways if they were no longer afraid of heavenly punishment. But he didn't act to ban it.

Sufficiently alarmed, Rieuwertsz continued to print the book, but in a more and more surreptitious manner, pretending the *Treatise* was a medical text, or a collection of essays by a well-known classical scholar. Even after the lynching of the De Witts, Spinoza's book was still available, though often under the counter, until July 1674, when the highest judicial court of Holland issued an edict against the *Treatise, Leviathan,* as well as Lodewijk Meijer's *Philosophy as the Interpreter of Holy Scripture* (see Chapter Five), books that

> undermined the teachings of the true Christian Reformed religion and in effect the authority of the Holy Scripture. . . . To prevent this harmful poison and to hinder as much as possible anyone from being misled by it, we have judged it to be our duty to condemn and proclaim the aforementioned

books as blasphemous and soul-harming books, full of ground-less and dangerous opinions and abominations that injure true religion and true worship. Accordingly, we hereby forbid everyone and anyone from printing, circulating, or selling, by auction or otherwise, such or similar books.[14]

The edict went out under the name of Willem Hendrik, by the grace of God, prince of Orange and Nassau, count of Katzenellenbogen, and so on—that is to say, Prince William III, stadtholder of the Dutch Republic and future King "Billy" of England, Ireland, and Scotland, until his death in 1702.

10

◆·◆·◆

Lonely at the Top

A FASCINATING PAMPHLET was published in Paris in May 1673, entitled *The Religion of the Dutch* (La religion des Hollandois). The book, it says on the title page, consists of "several letters written by an officer of the King's Army to a Protestant pastor in Bern."[1] The officer in question was Jean-Baptiste Stouppé, or Stoppa, or Stuppa, depending on which of the different languages of his native Switzerland was used. Stouppé, then, was a colonel in Louis XIV's occupation army in the Dutch Republic. He is often confused with his elder brother, Jean-Pierre, who was a military commander in Utrecht, where both men served under the duke of Luxembourg and the prince of Condé, one of the king's top generals.

The Stouppés were a Protestant family. The brothers were born in the Swiss canton of Graubünden, best known for the town of Davos. Jean-Baptiste, author of the pamphlet, had had a somewhat checkered career, first as a student of theology at

Leiden University, then as a Huguenot preacher in London, from where he also served as Oliver Cromwell's envoy to Cardinal Mazarin, Louis XIV's chief minister, before Cromwell suspected him of spying for the Spanish crown; Stouppé then enrolled in the French army and converted to the Catholic faith. Known as a rather slippery free spirit, with an interest in alchemy, Stouppé liked to observe: "No money, no Swiss."[2]

The pastor in Bern, named Hommel, had written a letter to Colonel Stouppé, criticizing him for taking part in the invasion of a good Protestant nation under the flag of a Catholic king. It was surely the duty of all born Protestants to take the side of the Dutch in this conflict. Stouppé's defensive reply to the pastor was couched as an argument that the Dutch Republic, far from being a good Protestant nation, was in fact a country of mercantile freethinkers and a hodgepodge of religions and attitudes including Catholics, Lutherans, Arminians, Quakers, libertines, Socinianists, seekers without any known faith, and even Persians and Jews. The Dutch didn't care much for outward pomp and ceremony. The moneybag was the only thing they thought worthy of worship. Stouppé went on to describe an extraordinary Dutchman with many followers, named Spinoza.

This Spinoza was "a very bad Jew, and no better a Christian," who had "opened the gates to atheism, libertinage, and freedom of all faiths." Stouppé relates, correctly, that Spinoza believed that the only use for religion was to "make citizens lead honest lives and obey their government," and that people "must be virtuous, not in the hope of being rewarded after they die, but because of virtue's intrinsic value, whose benefits can be enjoyed in the here and now by those who seek to be virtuous." Spinoza was clearly a learned man, with deep knowledge of the Hebrew language and Jewish thought. His idea of God, still in Stouppé's account, was "nothing but the force of nature, spread to all creatures" and not "a being endowed with reason, infinitely perfect and happy, as we believe." No theologian in the Netherlands had seen fit to contest Spinoza's "pernicious book" in print, from which Stouppé could only conclude that the Dutch either "believe in nothing . . . or share [Spinoza's] feelings, or they lack the courage to refute him."[3]

There are some errors in Stouppé's letters. He claims that Spinoza's *Treatise* was already officially banned in the republic, which it wasn't. And he underrates the stern orthodoxy of conservatives in the Dutch Reformed Church. But his description of Spinoza's views is reasonably accurate. It appears on the surface that Stouppé deeply disapproved and was keen to distance himself from them. Since he was man with a strong libertine bent himself, he might have felt this necessary, so as not to be tainted with Spinoza's dangerous ideas. And yet, even as his book was going to print, a letter was delivered from Stouppé to Spinoza in The Hague inviting him to come to Utrecht as a guest of the prince of Condé, who was longing to hear his views in person. Could it be that Stouppé was in fact an admirer of Spinoza, who had to disguise his interest behind a critical mask? A Dutch theologian named Johannes Braunius, who wrote a riposte to Stouppé's pamphlet and pointed out that the *Treatise* had been widely attacked in the republic, believed that Stouppé wanted to be friends with Spinoza. Colerus relates that there had been quite a lot of correspondence between the two, even before the invitation was sent out. Since it was forbidden to receive letters from the French occupied areas of the Low Countries, these were perhaps carried to The Hague by a sympathetic courier. The name of Everard Booth, son of the mayor of Utrecht, is mentioned. If such letters ever existed, they no longer do. Colerus also mentions that the prince of Condé had asked Spinoza to dedicate one of his books to the French king, in exchange for which an annual stipend might be arranged.

Louis II de Bourbon, prince of Condé, to use his full name, was himself a remarkable figure. After being compelled to marry Cardinal Richelieu's niece when she was only thirteen, he had made his name as a doughty warrior during the Thirty Years' War. In the Dutch campaign, he fought so hard in one notable battle that three horses were shot from under him. Yet this martial hero was also a man of some refinement. A freethinker, he hosted such distinguished writers as Racine, Molière, and La Fontaine at his chateau in Chantilly, outside Paris. His personal secretary was Isaac de la Peyrère, the man who argued that mankind long preceded Adam and Eve. Drawn to odd experiments, Condé once set fire to fragments of the cross that Christ was supposedly nailed to, to see whether they would burn. By the time Condé was posted in Utrecht, Spinoza's name as a radical thinker had spread all over Europe. It is easy to imagine why the prince, and his libertine courtiers, would wish to meet him.

Harder to fathom is why Spinoza would have wanted to meet French military officers who occupied parts of his native country, and whose armies had rampaged through the Dutch countryside with unspeakable cruelty. There is no sign that Spinoza ever considered dedicating his books to King Louis XIV, or indeed to receive money from him. Spinoza remained a staunch Dutch patriot who deplored the French occupation. And yet, despite his usual caution, his less than robust health, and his hostile feelings toward the French invaders, he accepted Stouppé's invitation, something one eminent Dutch writer on Spinoza described as "the most inexplicable event in Spinoza's life, so inexplicable indeed that people have doubted whether it ever took place."[4]

We know that it took place. The question is why. Some have speculated that Spinoza was acting as an envoy for the Dutch government to conduct peace negotiations. But this is improbable. Why should a government of Orangists entrust such a mission to a notorious philosopher and former supporter of Johan de Witt? A more plausible explanation might be that Spinoza was feeling increasingly lonely in The Hague. Some of his closest friends in Amsterdam had either died (Simon Joosten de Vries,

Pieter Balling) or left the country, or both (Franciscus van den Enden). Spinoza was also being attacked from all sides, not just by Calvinist preachers, which he had come to expect, but by people who might have warmed to his ideas. Things had changed in the Dutch Republic since the lynching of the De Witt brothers. Without True Freedom, The Hague had lost its political zip, and fawning over the House of Orange now set the tone. Even though Spinoza was never arrested, his position was precarious. He might have been intrigued by the prospect of meeting highly cultivated Frenchmen with whom he could have a serious conversation about philosophy.

Even after Prince William was installed as stadtholder, the political institutions of the Dutch Republic remained much as they were. The States General was still the main legislative body, and the provinces still had considerable autonomy. But William now had the authority to appoint his own people in local and national government. Regents on the side of the De Witts were purged and replaced by Orangists, even in the relatively liberal city of Amsterdam. The fact that William only visited Amsterdam three times between 1672 and 1684 shows how frosty his relations with the commercial capital remained.

The Orangist revival also strengthened the hands of orthodox Calvinists in church and academe. Along with the liberals in government, professors suspected of dangerous Cartesian, Socinian, let alone Spinozist ideas were purged from university departments. Even the relatively relaxed Calvinist followers of the Dutch theologian Johannes Cocceius were pushed out, lest they put more orthodox views in doubt. Liberal regents could no longer drag their feet to stop controversial books from being officially banned.

In such circumstances, intellectual courage becomes a rare commodity; most people run for cover. Hence the sorry fact that devoted Cartesians felt the need to attack Spinoza's ideas to deflect criticism from themselves. That Spinoza was aware of this is revealed in a letter he wrote to Henry Oldenburg in 1675, explaining why he had had second thoughts about publishing his *Ethics:* "Moreover, the stupid Cartesians, because they are believed to favor me, try to remove that suspicion from themselves by constantly denouncing my opinions and writings everywhere."[5]

One critical work, written by a Cartesian professor of logic in Utrecht named Reinier van Mansveld, entitled *Against the Anonymous Political Theological Treatise* (Adversus anonymum theologo-politicum liber singularis), found its way to the bookshops in 1674, after being circulated in manuscript for several years. Van Mansveld, who was not at all an orthodox Calvinist, but an advocate of intellectual freedom, had remarked that "in my opinion that *Treatise* should be buried forever in an eternal oblivion."[6] He did not get his wish, of course. Spinoza mentions Van Mansveld's book in a letter to his friend, Jarig Jellesz, with his customary disdain: "I've seen in a Bookseller's window the book the Utrecht Professor wrote against mine, which was published after his death. From the few things I read at that time, I decided it was not worth reading, much less answering. So I left the book lying there, along with its author. I smiled to myself that the most ignorant are generally the boldest and the readiest to write."[7]

Another Cartesian critic of the *Treatise* was Lambert van Velthuysen, a theologian, philosopher, and, for some time, a regent in Utrecht. He was not only an admirer of Descartes, but of Hobbes too. In a letter to a Mennonite physician named Jacob Ostens, Van Velthuysen pretends not to know who the author of the *Treatise* is, but then accuses him of destroying religious worship and "teaching pure atheism."[8] He also claims to detect a tone of sly malice in the book. After being shown this letter, Spinoza responds with the peculiar venom he usually reserved for people who accused him of atheism. He cannot tell whether Van Velthuysen's letter was written "from malice or from ignorance," but clearly, he "finds nothing in virtue itself, or in understanding, which delights him, and he would prefer to live according to the impulse of his affects, if one thing did not stand in his way: he fears punishment." Spinoza writes that he would prefer people like Van Velthuysen to "neglect my book completely, rather than to be troublesome by interpreting it perversely, as they usually do everything."⁹

As with Stouppé's letter, there may be a certain degree of dissembling in this exchange. Van Velthuysen was purged after 1672 as one of Johan de Witt's regents. Despite his disagreements with Spinoza, he may have been more sympathetic than he let on. The fact that he refused to identify the author of the *Treatise* was also a way of protecting him. And Spinoza might have protested his love of God a little too much, which isn't to say that he was being dishonest. He was entirely sincere in his contention that everything emanates from God with essential inevitability. More letters would be exchanged between the two men in later years, in a much more affable tone. Indeed, Spinoza and Van Velthuysen became quite good friends after they first met in Utrecht as fellow guests of the French officers who had invited Spinoza for a visit.

If Spinoza felt isolated in the increasingly illiberal Dutch Republic, this was at least partly self-inflicted. In February 1673 he received a flowery letter from Johann Ludwig Fabritius, professor of theology at the University of Heidelberg and adviser to Karl Ludwig, elector of Palatine, one of the German imperial states. It began: "His serene Highness, the Elector Palatine, my most gracious Lord, has commanded me to write to You, whom I had indeed not known until now, but who has been most highly recommended to his Most Serene Highness, and to ask whether you would be inclined to take up an ordinary Professorship of Philosophy in his renowned university."¹⁰

This was yet another example of dissembling. That the

elector, an enlightened nobleman, wanted Spinoza to teach at the university he had lovingly restored from the ravages of the Thirty Years' War was quite true. Karl Ludwig was the son of Frederick V, the "Winter King," and Elizabeth Stuart, daughter of James I. Having grown up in exile in The Hague, he was a devout Calvinist, but also such a firm believer in religious tolerance that he built a "Concordia Church" in his castle at Mannheim, open to members of all religions, including Catholics and Jews. Not only that, but he appointed a Jewish professor, named Jacob Israel, as professor of physiology and anatomy at Heidelberg.

Fabritius was, however, a much less tolerant figure. He studied in the Dutch Republic, at Leiden, but as a student of the orthodox Gysbert Voetius, the scourge of Arminians, Cocceians, Socinianists, Remonstrants, and other liberal Christians. Not only did he know perfectly well who Spinoza was, but he had expressed his feelings about the *Treatise* to a friend in 1671: "I shudder when I see such unbridled licentiousness being presented in a public display, and the Christian Religion itself and the Holy Scripture being so openly blasphemed."[11] Unlike Stouppé, who was genuinely curious about meeting Spinoza, Fabritius was probably carrying out the orders from his aristocratic boss with distaste.

He might even have slightly misrepresented Karl Ludwig's intentions. Fabritius wrote in his letter to Spinoza that he would have "the most extensive freedom in philosophizing, which [the elector] believes you will not abuse to disturb the publicly established religion." A resident French intellectual in Heidelberg named Urbain Chevreau, who had recommended Spinoza to the elector, believed that all Karl Ludwig had meant was that Spinoza should stick to philosophy and steer clear of theology. But Spinoza was sufficiently put off by the tone of Fabritius's warning that he decided to turn the offer down. In his return letter, he politely reminded Fabritius that he had already suffered enough from denunciations by his enemies while leading a solitary life without any official rank. How much more "would I have to fear them after I rose to an office of this rank?"[12]

Spinoza was worldly enough to realize the perils, for a free-thinking man, of getting entangled in the politics of an academic institution. Although not at all without intellectual vanity—on the contrary, in fact—Spinoza really did cherish his autonomy much more than the spoils of money and status. Again, this is why he resented being called an atheist, which he associated with unworthy material ambition. So, he ended his letter by saying: "You see, then, Most esteemed Sir, that I am not holding back because I hope for some better chance, but from a love of tranquility, which I believe I can in some manner maintain, provided I abstain from public lectures."[13]

Since there were no such strings attached to his invitation from the prince of Condé, Spinoza set forth on the rather perilous journey from The Hague to Utrecht in the summer of 1674. Some of the country was still underwater to stop the French advance. Special passes were necessary to cross the lines into French-held territory. And there was a constant danger of running into deadly skirmishes between Dutch and French troops. There is reason to believe that Everard Booth, the Utrecht mayor's son, was sent down to accompany him. Once Spinoza arrived in Utrecht, he was received with exquisite courtesy by the French officers. The prince of Condé himself, sadly, had been ordered by Louis XIV to go south to fight against Prince William of Orange (which is when he lost those three horses from under him), but the duke of Luxembourg assured the philosopher of the prince's warmest sentiments.

The social scene that Spinoza encountered in occupied Utrecht was peculiar. Dutch intellectuals, mostly Cartesians like Van Velthuysen, as well as the mayor, Cornelis Booth, enjoyed copious meals with the top-ranking French occupiers and conversed on intellectual matters while enjoying excellent French wines. There was a rumor that the prince of Condé shared with the Utrecht mayor a taste for scandalous books, such as *In Praise of Buggery* (De laudibus sodomiae) by Giovanni Della Casa, but since this book never actually existed, this story must have come from local patriots who disapproved of Franco-Dutch fraternization.

Lucas relates that Spinoza was not at all fazed by the elegant French officers. Indeed, Lucas writes, Spinoza's "courtesy was more reminiscent of a noble court than of a typical commercial city to which he owed his birth, but whose vices and flaws he did not share."[14] About Spinoza's politesse there can be no doubt; he was educated in the good manners of a high-born Iberian, after all. But the above description might have more to do with Lucas's French prejudice than with Spinoza's own disposition.

Even though Pierre Bayle believed that Spinoza did in the end meet the prince of Condé, who supposedly offered him a lavish stipend if the philosopher would agree to return with him to reside at Louis XIV's court in Versailles, there is no proof that Spinoza ever did. In which case, Spinoza's answer to the prince, namely that even the great power of his highness would be insufficient to protect him against the bigotry of the court, must be apocryphal as well.

How much Spinoza got out of his sojourn in Utrecht is unclear, but he did stay for three weeks, which may have been due to the difficulties of crossing a war zone to get back home. Spinoza's visit to the French had not endeared him to the citizens of The Hague. People whispered that he was an enemy spy, the kind of suspicion that is quickly leveled at unpopular outsiders. Memories of the lynchings were still raw. Spinoza's landlord, Van der Spyck, was worried that an angry mob might attack his house and murder his lodger. But Spinoza reassured him with the words: "Don't worry. I'm innocent. There are great men who know very well why I went to Utrecht. If you see people making trouble at your front door, I'll go out into the street even if I'd be treated in the same way as the two gentlemen De Witt. I am an honest republican and have always done my best for the welfare of our state."[15]

Which great men Spinoza had in mind, and why he went to Utrecht, cannot be known with any degree of certainty.

Still, Spinoza was never bereft of company, and he attracted some important new acolytes. These were all the more welcome, because he was frequently importuned by letter writers, whose uninformed criticism irritated him—a feeling he rarely tried to conceal. A provincial notable named Hugo Boxel, for example, wished to know what Spinoza thought of spirits and ghosts, and how long they hovered around. Spinoza answered almost instantly that Boxel's letter was most welcome since "I think that not only true things, but even trifles and imaginations, can be to my advantage."[16]

Spinoza's home in The Hague attracted a stream of visitors, some of whom must have considerably tried his patience. Quite a few were French libertines, who knew little about Spinoza's philosophy but were attracted by his edgy reputation as an atheist. One who made a special journey to The Hague was an epicurean poetaster named Jean Henault, described by Pierre Bayle as "a man of wit with a refined love of pleasure and an artful taste for debauchery," who prided himself on his atheism, a sentiment he displayed with "abominable affectation."[17] Henault's best-known sonnet was entitled *The Abortion* (L'avorton).

Two more interesting admirers were clever young men on the make, both born in Germany: Georg Hermann Schuller and a nobleman named Ehrenfried Walther von Tschirnhaus, lord of Kieslingswalda and Stolzenburg. Schuller studied medicine, and Tschirnhaus read medicine and mathematics at Leiden University, where they became fast friends. Tschirnhaus, who barely survived the plague years, fought in Prince William's army and distinguished himself later by inventing an algebraic formula known as the Tschirnhaus equation. He also found a way of producing porcelain to compete with Chinese wares and wasted a great deal of time on alchemy. He was a more formidable intellectual than Schuller, whose German prose, in the opinion of some, was as clumsy as his Latin. Both men were keen to get to know all the leading lights in European philosophy, cultivating learned contacts in London and Paris, as well as the Dutch Republic. Schuller was for a time the private tutor of the son of Jean-Baptiste Colbert, Louis XIV's chief minister of state.

Like all assiduous networkers, Schuller and Tschirnhaus were often the conveyors of higher gossip. Writing from London in July 1675, Schuller informed Spinoza that his old friend Oldenburg, as well as Robert Boyle, had formed strange ideas about Spinoza's character, but that Tschirnhaus thankfully had put them right on that score. In the same year, Schuller mentions that Tschirnhaus told Christiaan Huygens, his mentor in Paris, that Spinoza thought highly of him, and that Huygens wished to convey his highest respects to Spinoza too. Tschirnhaus himself, in another letter, warned Spinoza that the French scholar Pierre Daniel Huet was preparing a hostile essay against the *Treatise*.[18]

Still, most of their letters were more substantial and contained probing questions about Spinoza's theories about free will, infinite substance, and so on, which showed that the two Germans, unlike some of the French libertines, had a genuine interest in his ideas. Spinoza offered concise, but not always adequate, answers. He remained cautious about how much he was prepared to give away. Which makes his enthusiasm to publish the *Ethics* a bit puzzling. He must have known that this book was even more likely to inflame religious passions than the *Treatise*, especially after De Witt's death deprived him of official protection. Still, he traveled to Amsterdam in the summer of 1675 to discuss the publication with Jan Rieuwertsz.

This was precisely the time when the huge new Portuguese synagogue was inaugurated very near the spot where Spinoza grew up. We don't know whether or not he went to see the building, but he would surely have disliked its ostentatious grandeur. In the *Political Treatise* he was working on in the last years of his life (and failed to finish), he specifically said that a national church, to be administered by the state to promote charity, justice, and civil obedience, should be large and expensive. People should of course be free to build other churches too, dedicated to their own various faiths, but they had to be more modest. Nor would he have been pleased by the support given by many Portuguese Jews to Prince William, and even less by the attempts of some Jewish merchants to protect their interests by offering money to the French.

Away from the synagogue, Spinoza was spotted at a grand dinner by a liberal theologian named Philipp van Limborch, who remarked that Spinoza appeared to mock the other guests by laughing while they were at prayer, thus revealing his atheism. This seems out of character for a man of such natural courtesy. Perhaps a refusal to pray at all was already seen as mockery, even by a broad-minded Remonstrant. In any case, Spinoza wrote to Oldenburg in September that rumors about the publication of his *Ethics* had prompted Calvinist preachers to complain to Prince William about this scandalous prospect.[19] When friends warned Spinoza that he was asking for trouble, he abandoned his plan to publish the book.

One of the grand people contacted by Tschirnhaus in Paris was the famous German mathematician and philosopher Gottfried Wilhelm Leibniz. They shared intellectual interests, a passion for lens-making, and a taste for the high life. Leibniz was a brilliant, somewhat dandified young man who had made a name for himself by inventing a calculating machine, which he demonstrated to the Royal Society in London. As well as being well versed in philosophy, geometrics, and law, among other subjects, Leibniz was an ambitious diplomat who came to France to persuade Louis XIV to stop pestering neighboring European countries and to invade Egypt instead. He failed in this mission. Rather typical of Leibniz was his affectation of calling himself Baron G. W. von Leibniz, even though there was no evidence that he had any claim to this title.

Spinoza's fame or notoriety had reached Leibniz's keen ears early on. He sent Spinoza a letter in 1671, addressing him as "most profound philosopher," which began: "I have heard that one of the reasons for your great renown is your extraordinary skill in optics."[20] Enclosed with this letter was an essay on the subject by Leibniz, which he asked Spinoza to pass on to other illustrious Dutch experts. Spinoza's answer was polite but noncommittal. Clearly, Leibniz wanted to be in touch with the profound philosopher. What he didn't say was that he had read the *Treatise* quite carefully and deplored the fact that such a learned man "appears to have sunk so low."[21] Even as he was trying to ingratiate himself with Spinoza, he encouraged others to attack him.

Leibniz may have followed up on his first letter to Spinoza, but no correspondence has survived. In 1675 Schuller mentioned Leibniz in a letter sent to Spinoza from Paris. Their mutual friend Tschirnhaus, he wrote, thought very highly of Leibniz's moral character, as well as his excellent work on metaphysical matters to do with God and the soul. If Spinoza would be prepared to let Leibniz see a copy of the *Ethics*, this would surely be of great use to him. If not, Tschirnhaus promised to keep the contents of the book to himself. Tschirnhaus was sufficiently trusted by Spinoza to be given his own copy of the manuscript. Spinoza replied that he had had some correspondence with Leibniz and believed him to be a fine and learned gentleman, but considered it "imprudent to send him my writings too swiftly. I'd like to know first what he is up to in Paris."[22]

Spinoza was quite right to be wary of his young correspondents. Tschirnhaus failed to keep his word and did show the *Ethics* to Leibniz. (And in later years, Tschirnhaus also pretended that he had barely known Spinoza, and certainly hadn't been influenced by him.) The same copy, no one knows how, fell into the hands of Niels Stensen, or Nicolas Steno, the Danish anatomist who had already had friendly relations with Spinoza in his Rijnsburg days. Stensen had converted since then from his Lutheran faith to Catholicism. Outraged by the *Ethics*, he handed the "evil" manuscript to the Inquisitorial authorities in Rome in 1667.[23] He was ordained as a bishop in that same year. In 1988 Pope John Paul II beatified him.

Far from being a religious fanatic, Leibniz was intrigued by Spinoza's metaphysical ideas. Indeed, in the words of one writer on Leibniz and Spinoza, his interest in 1676 "began to take on the character of an obsession."[24] But this obsession would also be marked by a great deal of dissembling. A rationalist, he shared Spinoza's love of scientific inquiry and his disdain for miraculous enchantment. He later admitted that he once "went a little too far" in the direction of Spinoza's thinking.[25] But Leibniz was also a Christian who was unable to let go of God as the wise and omniscient creator of the best possible world. Even though Leibniz tried to reconcile these different ideas—he was a great reconciler; he even tried to unite Protestants and Catholics—he was never convincingly able to do so, which led to an endless argument with himself, but also with Spinoza. He pored over Spinoza's correspondence and added long commentaries to these letters, as though he were a rabbinical scholar, and Spinoza's missives the Talmud. Leibniz was fascinated by Spinoza's metaphysics and shocked by them as well. To accept Spinoza's idea of God was to reject the Christian, or indeed Jewish, God. This is one reason why Leibniz often pretended to be less influenced by Spinoza than he might in fact have been.

Leibniz also aspired to the kind of worldly honors that Spinoza consistently rejected: to be a member of the Royal Society and the French Academy of Sciences, to serve Louis XIV, and to be a courtier of the duke of Brunswick, a position he filled for much of his life. Leibniz was a formidable thinker, but it is difficult, and perhaps even impossible, to be a diplomatic operator without engaging in a certain amount of duplicity. In one of his commentaries on a letter by Spinoza to Oldenburg, he wrote: "A metaphysics should be written with accurate definitions and demonstrations. But nothing should be demonstrated in it apart from that which does not clash too much with received opinion."[26]

In November 1667 Leibniz boarded the yacht of Prince Ruprecht von der Pfalz at Sheerness in England. He was on his way to the duke of Brunswick's court at Hanover but wished to stop over in the Dutch Republic to meet various important thinkers, particularly Spinoza. In Amsterdam, he was introduced by Schuller to Lodewijk Meijer, Jarig Jellesz, and others in Spinoza's circle. Sailing down the canals in a well-appointed boat, he stopped in Delft to meet Antonie van Leeuwenhoek, the first man to discover microbes. Then he went to The Hague, where he finally met Spinoza. Leibniz liked to pretend that he bumped into the notorious thinker quite casually and only spent a short time with him. In private notes, he was more specific. He had spent several hours with Spinoza after dinner, discussing the murder of the De Witt brothers and other salient facets of Dutch politics. In another private letter, he was even more forthcoming and noted that he had seen Spinoza several times on his visit to The Hague, and "spoke to him at great length."[27]

Several hundred years later, a classical historian from Vienna named Theodor Gomperz pictured the scene with an air of plausibility. There in Spinoza's humble home was Leibniz, bewigged and "dressed in travel clothes of the latest fashion; great was his desire to shine, as his friend Huygens observed." And there, "already dwelling in the shadow of death," was Spinoza, "his body ravaged by illness, wrapped in poor clothing."[28]

The poor clothing was a kind of dressing gown, the type of comfortable garment many men wore at home, except that Spinoza's was not a silk "Japanese robe" decorated with birds, but a simple serge gown. They spoke in Latin.

Some of their discussion is reported in notes written by Leibniz after their meeting, and in his letters to a French friend. Leibniz began with criticizing Descartes's theory of motion— the idea, for example, that a thing, once moved, continues to move. He was surprised that Spinoza evinced so little interest in his critique. Another topic was whether God's existence could be proven. Leibniz thought he could do so. Spinoza was skeptical, but then offered some qualified agreement. The God Leibniz had in mind was an absolutely perfect being who created a world of perfect harmony. He found Spinoza's idea that God and the world were the same thing in substance "full of paradoxes." Spinoza, in Leibniz's view, failed to prove the existence of God.[29]

The two brilliant men might have been speaking at cross purposes. For they had different Gods in mind, one a perfect and wise providential God, and the other God as the embodiment of nature. Gomperz, the classical historian from Vienna, who described the scene of the legendary meeting so vividly two centuries later, expressed the contrast perfectly. He wrote that under the humble roof of Spinoza's home, "two eras in the development of the human spirit stood eye to eye. The extraordinary thing was that the old times were personified by the younger thinker, and the new times by the older man."[30]

11

His Last Breath

In the winter of 1675, Spinoza wrote a long and angry letter to a young man who had once been a keen student of philosophy. He was Albert Burgh, the son of Coenraad Burgh, one of the wealthiest regents of Amsterdam, a liberal-minded man with close ties to the Collegiants. Albert, whom Spinoza first met at Franciscus van den Enden's school, and later in Leiden, was highly intelligent but lost his way—in Spinoza's eyes, certainly—in the manner of many a pampered child of rich parents. During a sojourn in Italy, Albert decided to become a Roman Catholic, much to the consternation of his parents, and acquired all the fanaticism of the recent convert. Before making his way back to Amsterdam, barefoot and dressed in the rags of a mendicant friar, he wrote a letter to Spinoza full of the callow self-righteousness of a confused young man who believes he has suddenly seen the light. Once, he wrote, he had admired Spinoza for the subtlety of his mind, but he pitied him now, for he, Spinoza, had been "led astray and deceived by that wretched and very proud Prince of wicked Spirits. What is your whole Philosophy but sheer illusion and a Fantasy." He thought there was only one way out for Spinoza, that "wretched little man," that "base little earthworm" who fancied himself better than the "Incarnate, Infinite Wisdom of the Eternal Father." To save his soul, Spinoza should repent his sins and "realize the fatal arrogance of [his] wretched and insane reasoning."[1]

That Spinoza even deigned to reply was probably out of a sense of loyalty to Albert's father, who once stood by him at the time of his *herem*. Coenraad Burgh might even have asked Spinoza to talk some sense into the boy. How, Spinoza wonders in his letter, could Albert possibly know that he had found the perfect faith, if he hadn't even studied the world's other religions? That Albert's chosen religion was old and had many martyrs was an absurd reason to convert. After all, the Jews (Spinoza calls them the Pharisees) have always made similar claims. In fact, they are much richer in martyrdom than the Christians. Spinoza mentions the case of a certain Judah the Faithful, who sang psalms while succumbing to the flames on the stake of the Inquisition. He tells Albert to reject superstition and acknowledge the rational faculties that God had given him. He should cherish reason, if he didn't want to be counted among the animals who had to do without it.[2]

The reference to Judah the Faithful, in the waning stages of Spinoza's life, has prompted some speculation that he was looking back to his own religious roots. The unfortunate Judah was in fact a Christian convert to Judaism who had circumcised himself, an act that must have been almost as excruciating as burning at the stake. The fact that Spinoza calls him "the faithful" instead of "the believer," as Christians do, has been read as a sign of his Hebrew beginnings, because *creyente* (believer) and *fidus* (faithful) have no common root in Spanish or Latin, unlike in Hebrew.[3] Another distinguished writer on Spinoza believes that the Judah reference shows an "unusually fervent sympathy" for the martyr and could be a sign that Spinoza's "Judaic past began to reassert itself."[4]

Calling the Jews Pharisees is hardly a mark of warm solidarity. But it is true that Spinoza began to work on his *Compendium of Hebrew Grammar* (Compendium grammatices linguae hebraeae) around that same time. This was something he had been asked to do before by friends in Amsterdam. Hugo Grotius had already said in 1618 that Jews could benefit Christians by teaching them to read the scripture in Hebrew. Spinoza died before he could complete this project, but the way he went about it hardly suggests a desire to rekindle his ancestral faith. He approached the ancient language in the same way he studied everything else, systematically, by analyzing the laws underpinning Hebrew grammar. The conjugations of Latin were his model. As a result, he did to the Jewish tongue what he had done to the Jewish and Christian idea of God: he secularized it. He treated Hebrew not as a sacred language, or the language of rabbis, let alone of God himself, but a language spoken by ordinary people through the ages.

While working on his *Compendium*, Spinoza was already a very sick man. Years of breathing in glass particles had done his tuberculosis no good. He had become painfully thin, coughed all the time, ate very little, and a persistent fever kept him up at night. But Hendrick van der Spyck, Spinoza's landlord, spoke to Colerus of Spinoza's "unemotional and stoical attitude" and his low tolerance for people who treated their physical ailments with "cowardice and self-pity."[5] In his *Ethics*, Spinoza wrote the following proposition: "The free man thinks least of all of death. His wisdom lies not in his reflections on death, but on life." And the proof of this: "A free man, i.e., one who lives according to the dictate of reason alone, is not led by Fear, but desires the good directly from the foundation of seeking his own advantage.

And so he thinks of nothing less than of death. Instead his wisdom is a meditation on life."[6]

This is a very Spinozian statement, summing up concisely what he meant by *conatus*, the drive of all living beings to fight for their survival. Thinking about death is the domain of religion, whose rites and imaginings of an afterlife are aimed to reconcile ourselves to our inevitable fate. Spinoza's thoughts about his own end were practical and not philosophical. He asked Van der Spyck to make sure that his writing desk, containing his papers, should be sent immediately to Jan Rieuwertsz in Amsterdam. He still wanted his *Ethics*, which was among those papers, to be published as soon as possible.

If he didn't waste his time thinking of his death, what was Spinoza thinking of at the end of his life? The last thing he wrote reveals that far from being cast into a mood of melancholy fatalism, his mind was still actively engaged with the world outside his door on the Paviljoensgracht. Like the *Compendium of Hebrew Grammar*, he never finished his *Political Treatise*, but it is one of the most astonishing political texts of all time. It certainly was ahead of his own time.

Spinoza's beloved Dutch Republic was not moving in the direction that he would have welcomed. True, the French army had retreated in 1674 to the Spanish Netherlands, areas that are now in Belgium. This caused a rift between the merchant class in Amsterdam and the supporters of William of Orange, since the former wanted to end a ruinous war and return to business, while the prince wanted to continue pressing the French harder, with the help of Spain and the Holy Roman emperor. The prince got his way. By the time peace with France was finally established, William had turned abject defeat into a Dutch victory. In 1677 he married his cousin Mary, niece of King Charles II, which allowed the Dutch stadtholder to ascend the English throne after the Glorious Revolution of 1688. No wonder, then, that Prince William was seen as a savior by many of

his countrymen. The House of Orange was given the hereditary right to be stadtholders forever. One of the Dutch states
even wanted to give the prince full sovereignty. This didn't happen. The Netherlands remained a republic, but one that was
beholden to a quasi-monarchy. Spinoza was aware of the risks
involved in such an arrangement.

The *Political Treatise* repeats some of what Spinoza wrote in
his *Ethics*, as well as the *Theological-Political Treatise*, but in a far
more concrete, indeed practical fashion. He tried to explain the
failure of True Freedom and devise a theory of good government that could prevent tyranny from taking hold. Spinoza be-
gins by stating his opposition to utopianism. It is all very well
for philosophers to condemn human passions, vices, and weak-
nesses, and to devise abstract schemes for the ideal society based
on reason or human perfection, but such philosophical writing
has no practical purpose, since most people are neither reasonable nor perfect. Philosophers "conceive of men, not as they
are, but as they themselves want them to be."[7]

We must engage with people as they are, not just guided by
reason, but also by envy, hatred, treachery, greed, and other
passions. This is not a matter of good and evil, for there is nothing forbidden in the state of nature. Like the Marquis de Sade
a hundred years later, Spinoza didn't believe that man was bound
by morals dictated by God. But whereas Sade took this idea to
its logical extremes and painted a dystopian picture of unbridled lust and murder, Spinoza saw these natural human inclinations as the prime reason for building political institutions based
on man-made laws. The political state is essential to keep people safe from a war of all against all, and even though they will
have to be bound by laws, thereby giving up the freedom of nature, this is essential, since "men can hardly sustain their lives
and cultivate their minds without mutual aid."[8]

One fascinating aspect of the *Political Treatise* is that Spinoza makes no distinction, as far as base appetites are concerned,

between the common people and more cultivated citizens. He writes that this view "may be ridiculed by those who think the vices common to all mortals belong only to the plebeians—those who think that 'there is no moderation in the common people; that they're terrifying, unless they themselves are cowed by fear.'" Given that Spinoza himself warned against mob violence in his *Ethics* by using precisely those words, this is a remarkable statement.[9] Spinoza now claims that "everyone shares a common nature—we're just deceived by power and refinement."[10] But this apparent contradiction with earlier sentiments makes a kind of political sense. He is still terrified of the *vulgus*, and the violent passions to which it is prone, but in the *Political Treatise* he argues that everyone, however refined, can become part of the mob if the legal order breaks down.

The other weakness of abstract theory when it comes to politics is that it fails to take history into account. If Spinoza is guilty of this in his philosophical texts, he didn't make that mistake in his *Political Treatise*. Different places have different traditions. Old arrangements are hard to break down, and violent revolution, as he already argued in his *Political Theological Treatise*, usually begets more violence. So, Spinoza decided to assess the pros and cons of monarchy and aristocracy in more detail, as well as of democracy, which did not yet exist in his time, at least not in any shape recognizable to us. As he pointed out in his earlier texts, any viable form of government must be based on regard for the common interest. Without that, legitimacy is lost, and government will collapse.

One of the oldest questions in politics is whether people have the right to rebel. More than two thousand years ago, the great Confucian thinker Mencius said about rulers that "He who is cruel to the last degree to the people will himself be killed, and his kingdom will perish." He didn't speak of rights, but he considered it natural for an oppressed people to revolt. Confucius himself said that if a ruler "is not correct in his personal conduct, he may issue orders, but they will not be obeyed."[11] Spinoza would have concurred, although he would not have condoned violence. As a man of his time, he had an absolutist idea of state power. The ruler, whether a king, an aristocracy, or elected representatives, had the power to make laws, but need not be bound by them if it were in the common interest to break the laws. Citizens or subjects, on the other hand, did not have that right, even if they found the laws oppressive. Putting up with irksome laws was a lesser evil than lawlessness and disorder. But Spinoza conceded that if by breaking the laws the ruler weakened the state and provoked popular anger, "by that very fact the commonwealth is dissolved, and is inoperative."[12]

Spinoza once again made a strong argument against the desire for a monarchy. It was the worst of all systems, worse than aristocracy, because no king could rule entirely by himself and would need the help of cronies, thereby creating a hidden aristocracy. But if a monarch should rule a country, "he will be most his own master, when he's most attentive to the well-being of the multitude."[13] To make sure of this, the king must have many councilors, chosen from citizens with expertise and experience, who will serve for only a limited number of years. Since most people crave honors, it would not be hard to find candidates for the job. Their duty should be to defend the laws and offer the king advice, so he would know what to decree in the public interest—and that on the understanding that the king "will not be permitted to decide anything about any matter unless he has first heard the opinion of this Council."[14]

What Spinoza was proposing was not so very different from the kind of constitutional monarchy that came to the Netherlands, and other European countries, only during the nineteenth century. He had other ideas that would still be considered extremely radical in liberal democracies today. Land and, where possible, properties should be publicly owned, and countries should be defended by unpaid citizen militias. Spinoza was worried that too much economic inequality would weaken the state. He also thought that with a common stake in public property, people would have greater reason to defend it. This, then, was the proto-Marxian Spinoza that appealed to nineteenth-century socialists.

Spinoza also wanted to make it as hard as possible for the king's councilors to encourage military adventures. He was no doubt thinking about the recent wars favored by the Orangists. The councilors would surely be more inclined to choose peace if they knew that "their children and relations, occupied with private concerns, will be compelled to apply their zeal to arms and to go into military service. They can bring nothing home from that but unprofitable scars."[15] Again, many examples have more than vindicated Spinoza's opinion.

Turning to aristocracy, Spinoza writes with the Dutch Republic in mind once more. His definition of aristocracy describes the Dutch regents quite well, but not the French or English nobility. His idea of aristocracy is rule by a self-electing elite that governs cities and states with absolute authority. Membership of this patrician elite is not, however, a matter of birth but based solely on merit. Superior experience and expertise are the only things that distinguish patricians from the multitude. A supreme council should have the power to make the laws. A senate should guard the constitution and hold members of the ruling class to account.

Aristocracy is preferable to monarchy, because it is based not on one mortal person, but on institutions that outlive the men who govern them. But aristocracy shares with monarchy the problem of cronyism; rulers will be inclined to choose their own family and friends for high office, and to exclude people of greater merit. To guard against corruption, Spinoza wants the patriciate to be as large as possible. The bigger the population, the greater the number of patricians that is needed. Then they can carry the weight of governing, ensure stability, and reduce the chance of one clique hogging all the power. Reason would also be more likely to prevail, for a sufficiently large council would not be driven by "evil affects," since that would tear it apart. And it would not be guided by one mind, "except insofar as what they desire is honorable, or at least has the appearance of being honorable."[16]

Here, Spinoza was perhaps being a little too optimistic. But what he feared most, given the nature of the strife that dogged his own country, was sectarianism. Which is why he returned to his old hobbyhorse, a civic religion. Patricians, he thought, all had to be of the same religion, by which he meant faith stripped down to the cultivation of peace, charity, and justice. The republic of relatively flexible Dutch Calvinist regents under Johan de Witt conformed to some extent to Spinoza's ideal. Alas, however, in his view, there weren't enough of them, hence the end of True Freedom.

Spinoza addresses the critics of the Dutch Republic, who thought too much time was wasted on quarrels and disputes between different representatives of cities and provinces. He says there is nothing wrong with political debates; they are useful, indeed indispensable, in defining the common good. Nor is there any reason to believe that the republic couldn't endure without a noble stadtholder. Spinoza returns to his old argument that it is no good bringing down a ruler without changing the system of government. This didn't happen after De Witt dismissed the stadtholder, so most people were confused about the source of authority. More serious was the relative paucity of patricians, "far too few to be able to govern the multitude and overcome powerful opponents. The sudden overthrow of the Republic did not result from the fact that it wasted time in useless deliberations, but from the defective constitution of the state and the small number of its regents."[17]

Here, too, he was touching on a problem that is all too familiar to Americans today. Each province in the Dutch Republic, no matter how sparsely or densely populated, had the same number of representatives in the States General. This tilted political power away from the great merchant cities in Holland and toward the more conservative, rural, Orangist provinces of the republic.

Finally, Spinoza turns to democracy, which to him is the best form of government, because it avoids the patrician tendency toward cronyism and popular submission to the arbitrary will of small cliques unconstrained by the law. Democracy, to Spinoza, means that absolute authority rests in the hands of all citizens, for they have the right to choose the men who govern the state. Well, not exactly all citizens. The right to vote depends on national belonging, of course, so no foreigners, and on independence and respectability, so criminals and other disreputable types are to be excluded—as are children, slaves, and women, since they are dependent on their masters and husbands. Women are the weaker sex in Spinoza's opinion, and men only lust after them for their beauty. He also notes that men do not like the women they love to "favor others in some way." Therefore, he concludes that "men and women can't rule equally without great harm to the peace. But enough of these matters."[18]

These are the last words of the *Political Treatise*. Spinoza died before he could elaborate further on the political system he backed. That he should have ended on this particular note is unfortunate, given how strong feelings are on this matter in our own time. But since women only got the right to vote in the Netherlands in 1919, in the United States in 1920, and in France in 1944, perhaps one shouldn't judge a seventeenth-century philosopher too harshly.

Spinoza's last days were difficult, but tranquil. On February 6, 1677, the ubiquitous Georg Hermann Schuller wrote a letter to Leibniz, in which he said that Spinoza did not have much longer to live, as his "consumption—a congenital illness in his family—is getting worse by the day."[19] When Schuller visited him in The Hague, Spinoza asked him to go through his papers and destroy some of the more violent attacks on himself and his work.

Colerus heard from Van der Spyck the events of the weekend of February 20, 1677. On Saturday, the landlord and his wife went to their Lutheran church to prepare for Lent. After they returned in the afternoon, Spinoza came downstairs to smoke a pipe and chat about the day's sermon with them. He then lay down for a rest on the bed prepared for him in the front room. The next morning, before the Van der Spycks left for church, Spinoza spoke to them once more. A doctor identified by his initials L. M., most probably Spinoza's old friend Lodewijk Meijer, arrived and asked Ida van der Spyck to fetch an old hen to make some chicken broth. She did so, and when they came back from church in the early afternoon, Spinoza was sitting up having his bowl of soup with relish. They left him alone with Dr. L. M., so they could prepare for the Sunday evening meal in the church. When they returned that night, they heard that Spinoza had died at three o'clock in the afternoon in the presence of the doctor, who had already left by boat for Amsterdam. Some cash and a silver knife were missing.

Did Meijer take the gold coins and the knife with him as mementos? Or could it have been Schuller who later claimed to have seen Spinoza on his deathbed? In any case, Spinoza did not leave much in this world. There was his beloved parental bed, with a pillow, two cushions, and a red sheet; a few pairs of trousers and shirts, two black hats, a black "Turkish coat," two pairs of shoes, gray and black with silver buckles; a wooden contraption to grind glass and lenses; a case filled with books; a small painted portrait; four small tables of oak; and a suitcase. That was it.

An auction was held in The Hague on November 2. Among the items sold were books, papers, and bits and pieces of his glass-grinding equipment. The proceeds helped to pay for the funeral. But the most important manuscripts were already in the safe hands of Jan Rieuwertsz, who published *Ethics* as part of Spinoza's *Posthumous Works* (Opera posthuma) at the end of 1677. The reaction was harsh. Spinoza was attacked for undermining the belief in God. On June 25, 1678, the States of Holland gave out an order to suppress the *Posthumous Works* by all ways and means. More in the same vein would follow Spinoza's reputation for the next few centuries.

Spinoza dismissed any notion of an afterlife as superstition. When the body dies, the person ceases to exist. And yet, in his *Ethics*, Spinoza proposes something that appears to contradict this view. He writes: "The human mind cannot be absolutely destroyed with the Body, but something of it remains which is eternal."[20] Spinoza scholars have been trying to resolve this apparent contradiction forever. Some confess to being baffled.[21] Others dismiss it as rubbish.[22] Spinoza did argue that each extension of God, of which humans can only perceive bodies and thoughts, is unique and finite, but seen from the perspective of eternity, *sub specie aeternitatis*, we are part of infinite nature. To grasp this through reason, or a flash of instinctive insight, is to link up with eternity. In the words of Stuart Hampshire: "In our intellectual life, at the more successful moments of completely disinterested, logical thought, we have these glimpses of the possibility of living, not as finite and perishing modes of Nature, but identified or 'united' with God or Nature as a whole."[23]

I went to see Hampshire in the summer of 2004. He was very ill, lying in bed at his house in Oxford. His mind was still sharp as ever. We chatted a bit. Then there was a moment of silence. I could hear birds chirping outside his window, goldcrests perhaps, or robins. Suddenly the great scholar sat up in

his bed, and he said: "Spinoza was right!" I didn't quite understand why he was saying this. "It's all about biology!"

"I see," I said, still failing to get his point. Soon after, I said
goodbye to him, and that I hoped to see him again soon. "I
don't think so," he said. He died a couple of days later.

12

Spinozism

Benedict de Spinoza died in 1677, but Spinozism lived on, first in a stream of semi-clandestine publications and oblique references, much later as a full-blown cult, more powerful in our own time than ever before. The most recent Spinozists are neuroscientists who hail Spinoza as a proto-biological philosopher.[1]

The day after the thinker's death, his ever-busy acolyte Schuller suggested to Leibniz that his patron, the duke of Hanover, might sponsor a publication of the *Ethics*. This didn't happen. Leibniz didn't even bother to ask. But Schuller and Spinoza's Amsterdam friends quickly resolved to publish Spinoza's works, in Latin and in Dutch translation. They included the *Ethics*, the *Political Treatise*, the *Treatise on the Emendation of the Intellect*, the *Hebrew Grammar*, as well as the most important letters. The enterprise was not without risk. In an oversight that made Leibniz very anxious, Schuller failed to remove Leibniz's name from one of the scientist's letters to Spinoza. But Schuller reassured Leibniz that since the letter contained nothing but mathematical questions, he would not be compromised. The cover of the *Posthumous Works* only identifies the author by his initials, B. d. S., and the publisher (Jan Rieuwertsz, of course) is not mentioned at all.

Considering the immediate reaction from various political and church authorities, these precautions were only sensible. In June 1678 the city officials of Leiden, mindful of the many "shameful, Godless, and heterodox" views expressed in the book, which subverted "the entire Christian religion and would lead simple people to absolute atheism," decided that all copies be burned forthwith. The states of Holland and West Friesland took the same stern view. The "atheistic and blasphemous book" was duly banned, and those who defied the order were threatened with severe punishments.[2]

And yet Spinoza's ideas continued to percolate in various ways. Three years after his death, one of his former Dutch Cartesian antagonists said that "many men who are neither wicked nor stupid have become estranged from worship of the true God by Spinoza's arguments."[3] Even when his books could not be openly published, Spinoza's ideas were smuggled into a variety of texts, some in the form of fiction or travel tales. Translations of Spinoza's books in French appeared with bogus titles, such as *Treatise on Superstitious Jewish Rituals*. Intellectuals in Holland and beyond continued to discuss Spinoza's works. However, since Spinoza was officially demonized, his keenest followers often disassociated themselves from him in public, even as they promoted his ideas. If Heinrich Heine was right to see Spinoza as a Christ-like figure, his seventeenth- and eighteenth-century disciples behaved like Peter denying his knowledge of Christ three times before the rooster crowed.

Typical were such avatars of the French Enlightenment as Denis Diderot, who publicized Spinozist ideas, while making sure to cloak them in suitable words of disapproval. In the *En-*

cyclopédie, edited by Diderot, Spinoza is dismissed as a thinker of little consequence, and yet he gets far more space than many other important philosophers. The novelist George Eliot was among Spinoza's admirers in England. In 1854 she translated the *Ethics*. But she wrote to Charles Bray, a freethinking philosopher who believed that God could not be separated from nature: "By the way, when Spinoza comes out, be so good as not to mention *my* name in connection with it. I particularly wish not to be known as the translator of the *Ethics*, for reasons which it would be 'too tedious to mention.'"[4]

Like most Marxists, who have only a glancing knowledge of *Das Kapital*, Spinozists were not necessarily careful readers of Spinoza's books. Anyone with skeptical views about official church doctrine, whether Catholic or Protestant, was quickly tarred with the Spinozist brush. Jonathan Israel mentions the example of Julien Offray de La Mettrie, the eighteenth-century French physician, philosopher, and libertine who thought that human bodies were like machines or ships without a pilot, their actions determined only by the laws of nature. There was no such thing as a soul or a human mind detached from the body. He attacked Spinoza, was persecuted as a dangerous Spinozist, but, according to Israel, "apparently had no direct knowledge of Spinoza at all." What he conjured up was not the real Spinoza, or his works, "but the public 'Spinoza' which had become such a profound fixation of the countries he lived in."[5]

So, even though Spinozism for a long time resembled a secret cult, his ideas, even in a debased and often ill-understood form, had an enormous influence on the intellectual culture of Europe. The Enlightenment, of course, but also the political ideas that fed the French Revolution, as well as liberal democracy, socialism, and, in a perverse way, even fascism, all owed something to Spinoza's philosophy. To many nonreligious Jews since the Haskalah, or nineteenth-century Jewish Enlightenment, Spinoza also showed a way to reconcile their Jewish background with modern rationalism. The study of Hebrew as a secular language in the Haskalah followed his example.

But for a long time, the man, more than his works, appealed to the imagination of his many admirers. Even Pierre Bayle, who felt the need to be scathing about Spinoza's "pernicious and detestable" ideas, praised the honesty and simplicity of his behavior.[6] There was nothing studied or contrived about Spinoza's persona, but everything from his exotic appearance (exotic to the sturdy, rosy-cheeked burghers of northern Europe, at any rate) to his self-denial, his celibacy, and his message of universal salvation provided the perfect ingredients for the making of a secular saint, or at least the leader of a cult. This is where Heine's analogy to Christ is especially persuasive. Even the stories made up about Spinoza's death fit this description. According to Lucas, Spinoza died as if he were happy to "sacrifice himself for his enemies," so they could be cleansed of their calumnies.[7] He is also supposed to have uttered a variation of Christ's plea just before his arrest in the Garden of Gethsemane: "Oh, father, let this cup pass from me." When Spinoza realized he was dying, he is supposed to have said: "Oh, God, have mercy on this sinner!" Nonsense, according to Colerus, who mentions this story, but there are several reasons why people might have wanted it to be true: the final redemption of a godless man, or the human frailty of a saint, or the comeuppance of an unbeliever. Who knows?

It is not as a sacred idol that Spinoza speaks to us today, however, even though he is still often seen as a spiritual hero. In the preface to a new book on Spinoza in 1946, Albert Einstein wrote: "Although he lived three hundred years before our time, the spiritual situation with which Spinoza had to cope peculiarly resembles our own." The world was just emerging from the wreckage of a catastrophic war. Despite all the progress in the realms of knowledge and technological invention, mankind had descended to the worst kind of barbarism. The consolations of traditional religion, founded on authority, were lost. Modern man, Einstein wrote, had been banished "from a paradise of child-like innocence." Spinoza's reasoning, "the clear, precise formulation of his thoughts," and the "exemplary fashioning of his own life," would lead disillusioned modern man, if not back to paradise, at least to a release from "fear, hate and bitterness."[8]

The 1940s were an especially dark time, of course. But the spiritual situation described by Einstein is still with us. We, too, live in a period of extraordinary technological progress and expansion of knowledge. Almost everything we wish to know is only a click away on our phones or laptops. In most parts of the Western world, the traditional churches have lost their authority. And yet reason and freedom of thought are squeezed by many irrational currents, including the combination of political authoritarianism and religious bigotry that Spinoza would have recognized. The church was the main enemy of freethinking in his time. He believed that the emancipation from religious superstition by turning our rational faculties to secular affairs would liberate us from sectarian strife and intellectual oppression. That is why, in his view, the secular state had to wrest authority from the clerics and take charge of spiritual matters. What he did not see coming was that quasi-religious tyranny could arrive in secular guises. The despair of twentieth-century man that worried Einstein came from fascism, Nazism, and communism, state and personality cults that replaced organized religion with even more oppressive dogmas, celebrated with rituals and idolatry borrowed from the religions they tried to ban.

Émile Leon Cammaerts was an Anglo-Belgian poet. He coined the phrase: "When men choose not to believe in God, they do not thereafter believe in nothing. They then become capable of believing in anything."[9] They might believe quite harmlessly in Elvis Presley or the Maharishi Yogi, or, with far greater harm, in Stalin, Hitler, Chairman Mao, or indeed in

Donald Trump. Spinoza, if confronted with this phenomenon, would surely not have advocated a return to traditional religion, founded on authority. He might have doubled down on his idea of a common civic religion to foster charity and justice, without quite resolving the paradox of liberating people by enforcing obedience to an all-powerful state. But in our world of diversity, identities, and internet bubbles, it is in any case too late for that.

Einstein's insistence on clear and precise thinking, however, is still of critical importance. We must believe, with Spinoza, that there is such a thing as truth that can be pursued so long as we are free to use our capacity for reason. It is that freedom that is under threat, which makes the study of Spinoza more vital than ever.

When liberal journalists criticized policies of the Republican administration under George W. Bush, a Republican official famously replied that the critics were "in what we call the reality-based community." He defined this as people who "believe that solutions emerge from your judicious study of discernible reality." That, he argued, was not the way the world worked anymore, at least not from the point of view of the Bush administration: "We're an empire now, and when we act, we create our own reality."[10] The Trump era, when criticism was routinely called "fake news" and the president made things up as he went along, pushed this principle even further.

Creating their own reality is what totalitarian states do. They impose what people should think of the past, present, and future. But the right-wing attack on truthfulness echoes views promoted by some critics on the left. That people create their own reality is also the assumption of "progressives" who believe that all truth is but the reflection of relative power. It is taken for granted by some political activists and theorists that even to claim that there is such a thing as objective truth is just a way to disguise the assertion of social, political, sexual, or racial privilege. This assumes that someone born in a certain social class, or with a certain skin color, would necessarily hold a different view of truth than someone with another complexion or from a different class. This may sometimes be the case. We are all products of our own circumstances. But that does not mean that objective truth doesn't exist.

The disregard for the judicious study of discernable reality is not confined to any particular ideology. It is there on the right and the left. Hitler banned (and killed) dissident intellectuals because they undermined what he saw as *völkisch* reality—that is, the truth written in German blood. There was no such thing in the Third Reich as pure science; there was "German" science or "Jewish" science. To insist on the former meant eliminating the latter. Communist truth under Stalin or Mao was not based on race, but on a quasi-scientific view of history. If one didn't subscribe to the logic of communist truth, or the "natural laws" of political evolution, that the dictatorship of the proletariat would lead inexorably to the workers' paradise, one might be considered mad and locked up in a mental institution.

It is a very long way from Hitler's or Mao's murderous regimes to some of the intellectual shibboleths of our own time, but there are a few dangerous parallels. The insistence, for example, on "lived experience" as an essential condition of truth—that truth cannot be objectively acquired, let alone expressed, but is the property of a particular race or gender—is too close to the *völkisch* ideal for comfort.

Less fraught by a murderous history, but still anti-rational, is the idea that subjective feeling trumps discernable reality. Subjective feelings must not be dismissed; they are part of any "lived experience." Some people born in a male body feel trapped in the wrong gender and wish to live as women. One can respect this feeling without abandoning the biological truth that there are discernable differences between male and female bodies. Spinoza's insistence on separating theology from philosophy might offer a way out of these contemporary dilemmas. Subjective feelings exist, and so do biological differences. Both can be acknowledged, but they shouldn't be confused. Like theology and philosophy, they belong to different categories.

Freedom of thought is under threat from secular theologies, which insist, much like the church once did, on ideological conformity. There is no room for reasoned argument when views that don't conform to strict moral codes are regarded not just as untrue, but as sinful. Even scientific thinking today can be risky if it fails to affirm particular beliefs in social justice. This poses a similar threat to intellectual life that the church did in Spinoza's time, because it leads to timidity and conformism. Fear, as Spinoza kept insisting, is the enemy of clear thinking.

Much has often been made of Spinoza's personal caution, expressed in the motto engraved on his ring: "*Caute,*" or "Watch out." It is true, Spinoza was often careful. He stopped publication of the *Ethics* during his lifetime. He refused to have his *Theological-Philosophical Treatise* translated into Dutch. He was cagey about sharing his more provocative ideas with people he didn't know well enough to trust. But he was never a trimmer or a conformist. He didn't say one thing while meaning something quite different. Denouncing ideas he really believed in, as some of his followers did, would have run against his nature. Spinoza was careful, but never a coward. Once again, his defense of the freedom to think was absolute.

It is for this reason, and not for his Christ-like image, that Spinoza should be seen as a model in our difficult times, when the very idea of reason is regarded with so much suspicion by people who insist on the supremacy of moral beliefs. Closely linked to the idea of reason is the notion of universality. Not so long ago, many people in the Western world took it for granted that the capacity to reason was only the property of white Christian men; Asians, women, and other benighted members of the human race were incapable of it. Spinoza, with all his seventeenth-century notions of male superiority over females, never subscribed to that. Reason was universal, or it was nothing.

Was Spinoza a "good Jew"? In any conventional sense, he was not. He did not stick to Jewish customs and laws, and he did not believe in the Hebrew God. But his dedication to reason and freedom of thought, and his idea that these were universal goods, owed something, and perhaps even a great deal, to his being born as a Jew in a gentile society. One option for any member of a despised minority is to find some pride and dignity in the rituals and beliefs that separate your tribe from the rest of humanity. To divest oneself of these comforts is a dangerous thing to do. In Spinoza's time it was foolhardy. In this sense, he was not cautious at all, but extraordinarily brave. Since he was expelled from his tribe, one might say he had no choice. But of course he did have a choice. He chose to think freely, and that made his tribal membership impossible.

Spinoza was a man of many cultures, Dutch, Spanish, Portuguese, and Jewish. But he had no tribe. That made him a universalist. Other great thinkers born in Jewish families—Freud, Marx, Heine, et al.—followed his example. But their choices were easier than they were in Spinoza's time. Which is why they all, in their different ways, acknowledged their debt to him. Even if one does not accept that Spinoza was right about everything—how could he have been?—he showed the way in which all human beings can think freely and discover truths that apply to everyone. For that, we all owe him a debt, not as a "good Jew," or a secular saint, but as a great and humane man.

Chapter 1. Everyone's Spinoza

1. Quoted in Steven Nadler, *Spinoza: A Life* (1999; repr., Cambridge: Cambridge University Press, 2018), 141.

2. Hugh Aldersey-Williams, *Dutch Light: Christiaan Huygens and the Making of Science in Europe* (London: Picador, 2020), 318.

3. Quoted in *Scientific American*, October 11, 2018.

4. Heinrich Heine, "Zur Geschichte der Religion und Philosophie in Deutschland" (1834), in *Heinrich Heines Sämtliche Werke* (Berlin: A. Weichert, 1904), 51. Unless otherwise noted, all translations from non-English works are my own.

5. Karl Marx, *Critique of Hegel's Philosophy of Right*, quoted in Yirmiyahu Yovel, *Spinoza and Other Heretics: The Marrano of Reason* (Princeton: Princeton University Press, 1989), 82.

6. Feuerbach wrote this in his *Principles of the Philosophy of the Future*, quoted in ibid., 51.

7. Nadler, *Spinoza*.

8. Spinoza to Henry Oldenburg, October 1, 1665, in *The Col-*

lected Works of Spinoza, ed. Edwin Curley, vol. 2 (Princeton: Princeton University Press, 2016), letter 30. Here and throughout the book, I have relied on the translation from the Latin by Edwin Curley.

9. Yovel, *Spinoza and Other Heretics*, 30.

Chapter 2. The Safe Place

1. Jonathan Israel, *Radical Enlightenment: Philosophy and the Making of Modernity 1650–1750* (Oxford: Oxford University Press, 2002).

2. Quoted in Arthur Weststeijn, *De radicale republiek* (Amsterdam: Bert Bakker, 2013), 130.

3. Spinoza, *Theological-Political Treatise*, in *The Collected Works of Spinoza*, ed. Edwin Curley, vol. 2 (Princeton: Princeton University Press, 2016), chap. 20:40.

4. Quoted in Steven Nadler, *Spinoza: A Life* (1999; repr., Cambridge: Cambridge University Press, 2018), 13.

5. Quoted in ibid., 36.

6. Steven Nadler, *Rembrandt's Jews* (Chicago: University of Chicago Press, 2003), 190.

7. Yirmiyahu Yovel, *Spinoza and Other Heretics: The Marrano of Reason* (Princeton: Princeton University Press, 1989), 55.

8. Quoted in Henry Méchoulan, *Etre Juif à Amsterdam au temps de Spinoza* (Paris: Albin Michel, 1991), 30.

9. Ibid., 59.

Chapter 3. Born to Strife

1. Yirmiyahu Yovel, *Spinoza and Other Heretics: The Marrano of Reason* (Princeton: Princeton University Press, 1989), 30.

2. Quoted in Steven Nadler, *Spinoza: A Life* (1999; repr., Cambridge: Cambridge University Press, 2018), 71.

3. Koenraad Oege Meinsma, *Spinoza en zijn kring: Historisch-kritische studia over Hollandsche vrijgeesten* (1896; repr., New Delhi: Facsimile, 2019), 243.

4. Yosef Kaplan, "The Portuguese Jews in Amsterdam," *Studia Rosenthaliana* 15, no. 1 (March 1981): 41.

5. Quoted in Nadler, *Spinoza*, 87.

6. Ibid., 82.

7. Meinsma, *Spinoza en zijn kring.*

8. Ibid., 70.

9. Stuart Hampshire, *Spinoza* (Harmondsworth: Penguin, 1951), 16.

10. Meinsma, *Spinoza en zijn kring*, 51.

Chapter 4. Driven Out of the Temple

1. Jean Maximilien Lucas, *La vie et l'esprit de Monsieur Benoit de Spinoza* (1719), in *Die Lebensgeschichte Spinoza's*, ed. J. Freudenthal (Leipzig: Von Veit, 1899), 4.

2. Zbigniew Herbert, the Polish poet and connoisseur of the Dutch Golden Age, wrote a charming essay called "Spinoza's Bed" in *Still Life and a Bridle: Essays and Apocryphas* (New York: Ecco, 1991). He elaborated further on this tale by saying that Spinoza litigated against his sister for everything in his father's house, including the fire poker, before renouncing his claim to these useless objects.

3. Quoted in Koenraad Oege Meinsma, *Spinoza en zijn kring: Historisch-kritische studia over Hollandsche vrijgeesten* (1896; repr., New Delhi: Facsimile, 2019), 88.

4. Spinoza, *Treatise on the Emendation of the Intellect*, in *The Collected Works of Spinoza*, ed. Edwin Curley, vol. 2 (Princeton: Princeton University Press, 2016), chap. 2:6.

5. Spinoza to Jarig Jellesz, February 17, 1671, in ibid., letter 44.

6. See chapter 8 in Jonathan Israel, *Radical Enlightenment: Philosophy and the Making of Modernity 1650–1750* (Oxford: Oxford University Press, 2002).

7. Steven Nadler, *Spinoza: A Life* (1999; repr., Cambridge: Cambridge University Press, 2018), 125.

8. Ibid., 173.

9. Quoted in ibid., 103.

10. See, for instance, Frank Mertens, *Van den Enden en Spinoza* (Voorschoten: Spinozahuis, 2012).

11. Spinoza to Lodewijk Meijer, April 20, 1663, in Curley, *Collected Works*, vol. 1, letter 12.

12. Terentius (Terence), *The Eunuch* I.1, trans. Henry Thomas Riley, 1874, Perseus Digital Library, Tufts University, http://data .perseus.org/citations/urn:cts:latinLit:phi0134.phi003.perseus -eng1:1.1.

13. Spinoza to Lodewijk Meijer, April 20, 1663, in Curley, *Collected Works*, vol. 1, letter 12.

14. Quoted in Nadler, *Spinoza*, 172.

15. Quoted in Meinsma, *Spinoza en zijn kring*, 83.

16. Lucas, *La vie et l'esprit*, in Freudenthal, *Die Lebensgeschichte Spinoza's*, 8.

17. Pierre Bayle, *Dictionnaire historique et critique* (1697), in ibid., 30.

Chapter 5. The Dark Years

1. Quoted in Steven Nadler, *Spinoza: A Life* (1999; repr., Cambridge: Cambridge University Press, 2018), 140.

2. Ibid., 169.

3. Ibid., 150.

4. Ibid., 140.

5. This view has been pronounced in Odette Vlessing, "The Jewish Community in Transition: From Acceptance to Emancipation," *Studia Rosenthaliana* 30 (1996): 195–211.

6. This issue was still fiercely alive in 2021 when Rabbi Joseph Serfaty banned Itzhak Melamed, an Israeli-American professor, from entering the Portuguese synagogue to make a documentary about Spinoza. He declared Professor Melamed a persona non grata. This rabbi also refused to lift the *herem* on Spinoza in 2021. The board of directors thought the rabbi had overstepped the bounds of his authority and decided to dispense with his services.

7. Quoted in Yosef Kaplan, "The Portuguese Jews in Amsterdam," *Studia Rosenthaliana* 15, no. 1 (March 1981): 51.

8. Jean Maximilien Lucas, *La vie et l'esprit de Monsieur Benoit de Spinoza* (1719), in *Die Lebensgeschichte Spinoza's*, ed. J. Freudenthal (Leipzig: Von Veit, 1899), 8.

9. Spinoza, *Short Treatise on God, Man, and His Well-Being*, in *The Collected Works of Spinoza*, ed. Edwin Curley, vol. 1 (Princeton: Princeton University Press, 2016), chap. 2:2.

10. Spinoza, *Treatise on the Emendation of the Intellect*, in ibid.

11. Spinoza, *Ethics*, in ibid., pt. 4, prop. 8.

12. Ibid., pt. 4, prop. 17.

13. Spinoza to Henry Oldenburg, April 1662, in ibid., letter 6.

14. Margaret Gullan-Whur, *Within Reason: A Life of Spinoza* (New York: St. Martin's, 1998), 74.

15. Gilbert Ryle, *The Concept of Mind* (Chicago: University of Chicago Press, 1949), 13.

16. Quoted in Theo Verbeek, *Descartes and the Dutch: Early Reactions to Cartesian Philosophy* (Carbondale: Southern Illinois University Press, 1992), 55.

17. Ibid., 48.

18. Quoted in Nadler, *Spinoza*, 178.

19. Jonathan Israel, *Radical Enlightenment: Philosophy and the Making of Modernity 1650–1750* (Oxford: Oxford University Press, 2002), 28.

20. Spinoza, *Theological-Political Treatise*, in Curley, *Collected Works*, vol. 2, chap. 15:1.

21. Verbeek, *Descartes and the Dutch*, 37.

22. Ibid., 38.

23. Koenraad Oege Meinsma, *Spinoza en zijn kring: Historisch-kritische studia over Hollandsche vrijgeesten* (1896; repr., New Delhi: Facsimile, 2019), 318.

24. Quoted in Hugh Aldersey-Williams, *Dutch Light: Christiaan Huygens and the Making of Science in Europe* (London: Picador, 2020), 87.

25. Quoted in Meinsma, *Spinoza en zijn kring*, 216.

Chapter 6. Far from the Madding Crowd

1. William Canton to Margaret Fell Fox, 1657, quoted in Steven Nadler, *Spinoza: A Life* (1999; repr., Cambridge: Cambridge University Press, 2018), 190.

2. Quoted in ibid., 188.

3. Ibid., 192.

4. Quoted in W. N. A. Klever, "Spinoza's Life and Works," in *The Cambridge Companion to Spinoza*, ed. Don Garrett (Cambridge: Cambridge University Press, 2022), 23.

5. Spinoza to Henry Oldenburg, July 1662, in *The Collected Works of Spinoza*, ed. Edwin Curley, vol. 1 (Princeton: Princeton University Press, 2016), letter 7.

6. Spinoza to Henry Oldenburg, August 1661, in ibid., letter 1.

7. Spinoza to Henry Oldenburg, September 1661, in ibid., letter 2.

8. Henry Oldenburg to Spinoza, September 27, 1661, in ibid., letter 3.

9. Spinoza to Henry Oldenburg, October 1661, in ibid., letter 4.

10. Spinoza to Albert Burgh, 1675, in ibid., vol. 2, 76.

11. Spinoza to Henry Oldenburg, 1662, in ibid., vol. 1, letter 6.

12. David Vallins, *Coleridge's Writings: On the Sublime* (London: Palgrave Macmillan, 2003), 179.

13. Spinoza, *Short Treatise*, in Curley, *Collected Works*, vol. 1, pt. 1, chap. 10.

14. Stuart Hampshire, *Spinoza* (Harmondsworth: Penguin, 1951), 43.

15. Spinoza, *Short Treatise*, pt. 2, end.

16. Quoted in Koenraad Oege Meinsma, *Spinoza en zijn kring: Historisch-kritische studia over Hollandsche vrijgeesten* (1896; repr., New Delhi: Facsimile, 2019), 216.

17. Johannes Lindeboom, *Stiefkinderen van het Christendom* (The Hague: Martinus Nijhoff, 1929), 351.

18. Pierre Bayle, *Dictionnaire historique et critique* (1697), in *Die Lebensgeschichte Spinoza's*, ed. J. Freudenthal (Leipzig: Von Veit, 1899), 32.

19. Spinoza to Jacob Ostens, February 1671, in Curley, *Collected Works*, vol. 2, letter 43.

20. Simon Joosten de Vries to Spinoza, February 1663, in ibid., vol. 1, letter 8.

21. Spinoza to Simon Joosten de Vries, March 1663, in ibid., letter 9.

22. Spinoza to Henry Oldenburg, July 1663, in ibid., letter 13.

Chapter 7. Secular Salvation

1. Quoted in Koenraad Oege Meinsma, *Spinoza en zijn kring: Historisch-kritische studia over Hollandsche vrijgeesten* (1896; repr., New Delhi: Facsimile, 2019), 211.

2. Margaret Gullan-Whur, *Within Reason: A Life of Spinoza* (New York: St. Martin's, 1998), 152.

3. Spinoza to Pieter Balling, July 20, 1664, in *The Collected Works of Spinoza*, ed. Edwin Curley, vol. 2 (Princeton: Princeton University Press, 2016), letter 17.

4. Meinsma, *Spinoza en zijn kring*, 226.

5. Spinoza to Johannes Bouwmeester, June 1665, in Curley, *Collected Works*, vol. 2, letter 28. This letter is dated June 1665. Most experts believe the recipient was Johannes Bouwmeester, but one distinguished scholar, Koenraad Oege Meinsma, believes it might have been another friend, Adriaan Koerbagh. The reason he gives is Spinoza's request for a conserve of crushed rosebuds that would benefit his health. Since Koerbagh had written about such a conserve in a book, Meinsma assumes that this reference points to him as the recipient of Spinoza's letter. It seems a rather tenuous assumption.

6. June 1667 diary entry, in *The Diary of Samuel Pepys* (London: J. M. Dent, 1953), 481.

7. Spinoza to Henry Oldenburg, October 1, 1665, in Curley, *Collected Works*, vol. 2, letter 30.

8. Spinoza, *Theoretical-Political Treatise*, in ibid., vol. 2, intro:34.

9. Quoted in Steven Nadler, *A Book Forged in Hell: Spinoza's Scandalous Treatise and the Birth of the Secular Age* (Princeton: Princeton University Press, 2013), 30.

10. Quoted in Gullan-Whur, *Within Reason*, 200.

11. Spinoza, *Theoretical-Political Treatise*, chap. 14:5.

12. Ibid., chap. 3:16.

13. Ibid., chap. 3:53.

14. Gullan-Whur, *Within Reason*, 202.

15. Spinoza, *Theoretical-Political Treatise*, chap. 1:23.

16. Gullan-Whur, *Within Reason*, 284.

17. Spinoza, *Theoretical-Political Treatise*, chap. 5:3.

18. Ibid., chap. 4:6.

19. Ibid., chap. 15:37.

20. Stuart Hampshire, *Spinoza* (Harmondsworth: Penguin, 1951), 28.

21. Quoted in Jonathan Israel, *Radical Enlightenment: Philosophy and the Making of Modernity 1650–1750* (Oxford: Oxford University Press, 2002), 174.

Chapter 8. Radical Enlightenment

1. Steven Nadler, *Spinoza: A Life* (1999; repr., Cambridge: Cambridge University Press, 2018), 221.

2. Jonathan Israel, *Radical Enlightenment: Philosophy and the Making of Modernity 1650–1750* (Oxford: Oxford University Press, 2002), 278.

3. Margaret Gullan-Whur, *Within Reason: A Life of Spinoza* (New York: St. Martin's, 1998), 172.

4. Hugh Aldersey-Williams, *Dutch Light: Christiaan Huygens and the Making of Science in Europe* (London: Picador, 2020), 413.

5. Israel, *Radical Enlightenment*.

6. Arthur Weststeijn, *De radikale republiek* (Amsterdam: Bakker, 2013), 64.

7. Quoted in W. N. A. Klever, "Spinoza's Life and Works," in *The Cambridge Companion to Spinoza*, ed. Don Garrett (Cambridge: Cambridge University Press, 2022), 35.

8. Quoted in Koenraad Oege Meinsma, *Spinoza en zijn kring: Historisch-kritische studia over Hollandsche vrijgeesten* (1896; repr., New Delhi: Facsimile, 2019), 283.

9. Ibid., 301.

10. Quoted in Hannah Laurens, *De rede: Bron van geluk voor iedereen* (Nijmegen: Vantilt, 2019), 93.

11. Quoted in ibid., 94.

12. Quoted in Meinsma, *Spinoza en zijn kring*, 319.

13. *The Diary of Samuel Pepys* (London: J. M. Dent, 1953), 281.

14. Spinoza, *Theoretical-Political Treatise*, in Curley, *Collected Works*, vol. 2, intro:12.

15. Ibid., 18:32.

16. Ibid., 16:29.

17. Ibid., 20:35.

18. Ibid., 18:9.

19. Ibid., 4:27.

Chapter 9. Mob Rage

1. Jean Baptiste Stouppé, *La religion des Hollandois* (1673), in *Die Lebensgeschichte Spinoza's*, ed. J. Freudenthal (Leipzig: Von Veit, 1899), 195.

2. Quoted in Margaret Gullan-Whur, *Within Reason: A Life of Spinoza* (New York: St. Martin's, 1998), 225.

3. Spinoza to Jarig Jellesz, February 17, 1671, in *The Collected Works of Spinoza*, ed. Edwin Curley, vol. 2 (Princeton: Princeton University Press, 2016), letter 44.

4. Spinoza, *Ethics*, in ibid., pt. 4, prop. 45.

5. Ibid., pt. 4, prop. 18.

6. Ibid., pt. 4, prop. 46.

7. Ibid., pt. 4, prop. 65.

8. Ibid., pt. 5, prop. 42.

9. Ibid., pt. 4, prop. 54.

10. Quoted in Luc van Panhuysen, *De Ware Vrijheid* (Amsterdam: Olympus, 2018), 438.

11. Don Garrett, ed., *The Cambridge Companion to Spinoza* (Cambridge: Cambridge University Press, 1996), 40.

12. Jean Maximilien Lucas, *La vie et l'esprit de Monsieur Benoit de Spinoza* (1719), in Freudenthal, *Die Lebensgeschichte Spinoza's*, 19.

13. Quoted in Steven Nadler, *A Book Forged in Hell: Spinoza's Scandalous Treatise and the Birth of the Secular Age* (Princeton: Princeton University Press, 2013), 221.

14. Quoted in Freudenthal, *Die Lebensgeschichte Spinoza's*, 139.

Chapter 10. Lonely at the Top

1. Jean Baptiste Stouppé, *La religion des Hollandois* (Cologne: Pierre Marteaux, 1673).

2. Quoted in *De Gids* (Amsterdam), 1869, 182.

3. Quoted in Koenraad Oege Meinsma, *Spinoza en zijn kring: Historisch-kritische studia over Hollandsche vrijgeesten* (1896; repr., New Delhi: Facsimile, 2019), 367.

4. Ibid., 370.

5. Spinoza to Henry Oldenburg, September/October 1675, in *The Collected Works of Spinoza*, ed. Edwin Curley, vol. 2 (Princeton: Princeton University Press, 2016), letter 68.

6. Quoted in Steven Nadler, *Spinoza: A Life* (1999; repr., Cambridge: Cambridge University Press, 2018), 342.

7. Spinoza to Jarig Jellesz, June 2, 1674, in Curley, *Collected Works*, vol. 2, letter 50.

8. Lambert van Velthuysen to Jacob Ostens, January 24, 1671, in ibid., letter 42.

9. Spinoza to Jacob Ostens, February 1671, in ibid., letter 43.

10. Johann Ludwig Fabritius to Spinoza, February 1673, in ibid., 396.

11. Johann Ludwig Fabritius was reported to have said this. The quotation is in ibid., 364.

12. Spinoza to Johann Ludwig Fabritius, March 30, 1673, in ibid., letter 48.

13. Ibid.

14. Maximilien Lucas quoted in J. Freudenthal, ed., *Die Lebensgeschichte Spinoza's* (Leipzig: Von Veit, 1899), 16.

15. Quoted in ibid., 65.

16. Spinoza to Hugo Boxel, September 16–20, 1674, in Curley, *Collected Works*, vol. 2, letter 52.

17. Quoted in Freudenthal, *Die Lebensgeschichte Spinoza's*, 33.

18. Georg Hermann Schuller to Spinoza, July 1675; Schuller to Spinoza, November 14, 1675; Ehrenfried Walther von Tschirnhaus to Spinoza, May 2, 1676, all in Curley, *Collected Works*, vol. 2, letters 63, 70, 80.

19. Spinoza to Henry Oldenburg, September 1675, in ibid., letter 62.

20. Gottfried Wilhelm Leibniz to Spinoza, October 5, 1671, in Curley, *Collected Works*, vol. 2, letter 45.

21. Quoted in Jonathan Israel, *Radical Enlightenment: Philosophy and the Making of Modernity 1650–1750* (Oxford: Oxford University Press, 2002), 503.

22. Georg Hermann Schuller to Spinoza, November 14, 1675; Spinoza to Schuller, November 18, 1675, both in Curley, *Collected Works*, vol. 2, letters 70 and 72.

23. Matthew Stewart, *The Courtier and the Heretic: Leibniz, Spinoza, and the Fate of God in the Modern World* (New York: W. W. Norton, 2007), 187. A copy of this document was discovered in 2011 in the Vatican Library by a Dutch scholar named Leen Spruit. It is the only extant manuscript copy of the *Ethics* that we know of.

24. Ibid., 193.

25. Ibid., 195.

26. Quoted in Meinsma, *Spinoza en zijn kring*, 424.

27. Nadler, *Spinoza*, 398.

28. Theodor Gomperz, "Leibniz und Spinoza: Ein Vorwurf für Historienmaler," an article published in 1888 in *Die Nation, Wochenschrift für Politik, Volkswirtschaft und Litteratur*, quoted in Meinsma, *Spinoza en zijn kring*, 425.

29. Ibid., 424.

30. Quoted in ibid., 425.

Chapter 11. His Last Breath

1. Albert Burgh to Spinoza, September 11, 1675, in *The Collected Works of Spinoza*, ed. Edwin Curley, vol. 2 (Princeton: Princeton University Press, 2016), letter 67.

2. Spinoza to Albert Burgh, end of 1675/beginning of 1676, in ibid., letter 76.

3. See Yirmiyahu Yovel, *Spinoza and Other Heretics: The Marrano of Reason* (Princeton: Princeton University Press, 1989), 187.

4. Margaret Gullan-Whur, *Within Reason: A Life of Spinoza* (New York: St. Martin's, 1998), 285.

5. Johannes Colerus quoted in J. Freudenthal, ed., *Die Le-bensgeschichte Spinoza's* (Leipzig: Von Veit, 1899), 97.

6. Spinoza, *Ethics*, in Curley, *Collected Works*, vol. 2, 4:67.

7. Spinoza, *A Political Treatise*, trans. A. H. Gosset (London: G. Bell, 1883), chap. 1:1.

8. Ibid., chap. 2:15.

9. The phrase about the mob that has no fear being frightful comes from Tacitus, but is quoted by Spinoza in *Ethics*, 4:54. I am indebted to Steven Nadler for pointing this out.

10. Spinoza, *Political Treatise*, chap. 7:27.

11. Both quotations are from Gilbert Reid, "Revolution as Taught by Confucianism," *International Journal of Ethics* 33, no. 2 (January 1923): 144.

12. Spinoza, *Political Treatise*, chap. 4:6.

13. Ibid., chap. 6:8.

14. Ibid., chap. 6:17.

15. Ibid., chap. 7:7.

16. Ibid., chap. 8:6.

17. Ibid., chap. 9:14.

18. Ibid., chap. 11:4.

19. Georg Hermann Schuller to Gottfried Wilhelm Leibniz, February 6, 1677, quoted in Freudenthal, *Die Lebensgeschichte Spinoza's*, 202.

20. Spinoza, *Ethica*, intro. by Guido van Suchtelen (Amsterdam: Wereldbibliotheek, 1979), 8.

21. Edwin Curley, for example. See his *Behind the Geometrical Method* (Princeton: Princeton University Press, 1988).

22. See Jonathan Bennett, *A Study of Spinoza's Ethics* (Cambridge: Cambridge University Press, 1984).

23. Stuart Hampshire, *Spinoza* (Harmondsworth: Penguin, 1951), 175.

Chapter 12. Spinozism

1. Antonio Damasio, for example. See his *Looking for Spinoza: Joy, Sorrow and the Feeling Brain* (New York: Harcourt, 2003). See also Koenraad Oege Meinsma, *Spinoza en zijn kring: Historisch-*

kritische studia over Hollandsche vrijgeesten (1896; repr., New Delhi: Facsimile, 2019), 448.

2. Jonathan Israel, *Radical Enlightenment: Philosophy and the Making of Modernity 1650–1750* (Oxford: Oxford University Press, 2002), 307.

3. Quoted in Margaret Gullan-Whur, *Within Reason: A Life of Spinoza* (New York: St. Martin's, 1998), 310.

4. George Eliot to Charles Bray, 1854, quoted in ibid.

5. Israel, *Radical Enlightenment*, 707.

6. Pierre Bayle, *Dictionnaire historique et critique* (1697), in *Die Lebensgeschichte Spinoza's*, ed. J. Freudenthal (Leipzig: Von Veit, 1899), 30.

7. Ibid., 24.

8. Albert Einstein, preface to Rudolf Kaiser, *Spinoza: Portrait of a Spiritual Hero* (New York: Philosophical Library, 1946), ix.

9. The quotation, often attributed to G. K. Chesterton, but in fact coined by Cammaerts, appears in his *The Laughing Prophet: The Seven Virtues and G. K. Chesterton* (London: Methuen, 1937), 1.

10. Reported by Ron Suskind in the *New York Times Magazine*, October 17, 2004.

ACKNOWLEDGMENTS

MANY PEOPLE HAVE BEEN HELPFUL to me in the course of writing this book. I would like to thank some who have been especially supportive. Steven Nadler went out of his way to offer expert advice and prevent me from making the most egregious mistakes. Kees Schuyt, author of an excellent book on Spinoza's philosophy, generously allowed me to browse in his vast library of Spinoziana and offered invaluable insights. Avishai Margalit and Arnon Grunberg kindly read various chapters in progress. As did Phillip Blumberg; it is hard to imagine a better and more sympathetic reader. Gary Schwartz accompanied me to the Portuguese cemetery in Ouderkerk. Hanca Leppink and Hans Baaij helped me with introductions in Amsterdam. Emile Schrijver showed me around Ets Haim, the great library at the Portuguese synagogue in Amsterdam. Steven Zipperstein and Ileene Smith were the most encouraging editors. Heather Gold and Elizabeth Sylvia were most helpful in preparing the manuscript, and Laura Hensley did an outstanding job on the final copy.

INDEX

France (*continued*)
population in, 13; revolution in,
7, 168; voting rights for women
in, 162
Frederik Hendrik (prince of Orange),
36–37
freedom: democracy and, 10, 52, 118;
during Dutch Golden Age, 61,
117; intellectual, 9, 97, 98, 121,
141; of nature, 157; political
theory on trade and, 16; of
speech, 2–3, 101, 111; *Theological-
Political Treatise* on, 117–18; of
thought, 9, 67–68, 73, 90–91,
100–101, 108, 118, 170–74. *See
also* True Freedom government
free will, 72, 90, 128, 147
French Enlightenment, 167
French Revolution, 7, 168
Freud, Sigmund, 8, 12, 174

gedogen (tolerance policy): books and,
111; Cartesian ideas and, 73;
Cocceians on, 72; intellectual
gatherings and, 48; limitations
of, 117; modern examples of, 19;
Spinoza and, 77. *See also* religious
tolerance
Germany: Enlightenment in, 7; Jewish
population in, 13, 15, 25; Nazism
in, 3, 6–7, 10, 14, 22, 170
Geulincx, Arnold, 74
ghettos for Jews, 13, 15, 18, 21–22
Glazemaker, Jan, 77
Glorious Revolution, 156
God: corporality of, 55, 57; Descartes
on, 90, 127–28; existence of, 3,
84, 152; knowledge of, 84, 86, 90,
101; Leibniz on, 152; Maimonides on, 55; nature in relation to,
7, 67–68, 85, 110, 128; omniscience of, 33, 150; Spinoza on,
3, 7, 57, 66–68, 84–88, 128, 152;
truth of, 73, 75, 101
Goethe, Johann Wolfgang von, 7, 76
Golden Age. *See* Dutch Golden Age

Gomarus, Franciscus and Gomarists,
19–20, 35, 71, 134
Gomperz, Theodor, 151, 152
Goyen, Jan van, 3–4
Graevius, Johann Georg, 164
Grotius, Hugo, 17, 20, 21, 121, 155
Grunberg, Arnon, 11
Gullan-Whur, Margaret, 103

The Hague: atmosphere of, 107,
124; Domus Spinozana in, 4–6;
French influences in, 124, 125;
Jewish population in, 3; mob
violence in, 131–33; Spinoza's
burial in, 1–2, 132
Halevy, Moses Uriel, 17
Hals, Frans, 35
Hampshire, Stuart, 41, 85, 105, 164–65
Haskalah (Jewish Enlightenment),
168–69
Heereboord, Adriaan, 73–75
Heidanus, Abraham, 73
Heine, Heinrich, 7–8, 12, 104, 167,
169, 174
Henault, Jean, 146
Henrietta Maria (queen of England),
36–37
Herbert, Zbigniew, 177n2
herem. See banishment from Jewish
community
heresy and heretics: Arminians, 20;
banishment of, 57, 65; da Costa,
38, 41; Descartes, 54, 71; Remon-
strants, 71; Socinianists, 33, 71;
Spinoza, 3, 64, 66
Hess, Moses, 11, 12
Hinduism, 86–87
Hitler, Adolf, 170, 172
Hobbes, Thomas: atheism and, 99;
On the Citizen, 99; influence on
Spinoza, 52, 74, 111; *Leviathan*,
99, 134–35; Oldenburg's relationship with, 83; on sovereign
power, 118, 119; on Spinoza's
writings, 100
Holocaust, 11, 14, 22

Julius Rosenwald: Repairing the World, by Hasia R. Diner
Mark Rothko: Toward the Light in the Chapel, by Annie Cohen-Solal
Ruth: A Migrant's Tale, by Ilana Pardes
Gershom Scholem: Master of the Kabbalah, by David Biale
Bugsy Siegel: The Dark Side of the American Dream,
    by Michael Shnayerson
Solomon: The Lure of Wisdom, by Steven Weitzman
Steven Spielberg: A Life in Films, by Molly Haskell
Spinoza: Freedom's Messiah, by Ian Buruma
Alfred Stieglitz: Taking Pictures, Making Painters, by Phyllis Rose
Barbra Streisand: Redefining Beauty, Femininity, and Power,
    by Neal Gabler
Henrietta Szold: Hadassah and the Zionist Dream,
    by Francine Klagsbrun
Leon Trotsky: A Revolutionary's Life, by Joshua Rubenstein
Warner Bros: The Making of an American Movie Studio,
    by David Thomson
Elie Wiesel: Confronting the Silence, by Joseph Berger

FORTHCOMING TITLES INCLUDE:

Abraham, by Anthony Julius
Hannah Arendt, by Masha Gessen
The Ba'al Shem Tov, by Ariel Mayse
Walter Benjamin, by Peter Gordon
Franz Boas, by Noga Arikha
Bob Dylan, by Sasha Frere-Jones
Anne Frank, by Ruth Franklin
George Gershwin, by Gary Giddins
Ruth Bader Ginsburg, by Jeffrey Rosen
Jesus, by Jack Miles
Josephus, by Daniel Boyarin